Knitting as a Spiritual Path

Knitting as a Spiritual Path

Exploring a Wiser, Kinder, More Meaningful Life

~ One Stitch at a Time ~

SUSAN H. SWETNAM

Knitting as a Spiritual Path
Exploring a Wiser, Kinder, More Meaningful Life, One Stitch at a Time
by Susan H. Swetnam

Edited by Gregory F. Augustine Pierce
Designed and typeset by Andrea Reider
Image credits and sources listed on page 159

Published by ACTA Publications, www.actapublications.com, 800-397-2282.

Library of Congress Catalog number: 2022949212
ISBN: 978-0-87946-704-3
Printed in the United States of America by Total Printing Systems
Year 30 29 28 27 26 25 24 23 22
Printing 10 9 8 7 6 5 4 3 2 First
Text printed on 30% post-consumer recycled paper

Contents

Introduction 1
Knitting as a Spiritual Path 1

"Let Us Assert Ourselves" 13
The Path of Risk and Growth

Knitting Alone 27
The Path of Stillness

Knitting with Others 41
The Path of Fellowship

Knitting in Public 55
The Path of Equanimity

Knitting Gifts for Other People 69
The Path of Persistent Love

Knitters are Rippers 83
The Path of Humility and Imperfection

So Many Good Ways to Knit 95
The Path of Sacred Individuality

"And the World Will Live as One" 109
The Path of Cross-Cultural Understanding

Knitting and Nature 125
The Path of Awareness and Celebration

"All Great Works of Art Are Annunciations" 139
The Path of Joyful Co-Creation

Afterword 153
One Stitch at a Time

About the Author and the Images 159

This book is dedicated to my grandmother,
Elizabeth Shoemaker Rothenberger,
1899-2002
Faithful member and president
of the Ambler Knitting Guild
of Pennsylvania.

Beautiful knitter.
Beautiful person.

Introduction

Knitting As a Spiritual Path

The woman in the fourteenth-century painting has made good progress on her knitting project, what looks to be a stockinette-stitch garment fashioned in the round on four double-pointed needles, a technique still familiar to us who knit today. She's seated in a comfortable garden/patio setting, paying quiet attention to those slippery needles while also keeping an eye on her little son, who's reclining at her feet. Two adults stand to her left, friendly and smiling, visiting with her.

Paintings of women knitting have been common in western art since the Renaissance—a fact that may come as a surprise today, given that the practice is considered an everyday domestic craft. Yet museums around the world hold images of serene housewives and lovely young girls immersed in their needlework, painted by artists famous (Picasso) and lesser known (Dutch artists in the 1600s).

The woman in the painting on the next page, though, isn't just any serene housewife or lovely young girl going about ordinary business. As the visual attributions (including the halos) make clear, she's the Blessed Mother. People viewing that painting in its contemporary context would have understood that the child was Jesus and those friendly visitors were angels. This artist has chosen, in other words, to depict the woman whom Christians honor as the mother of God incarnate as a very competent knitter and her craft as something suitable for her attention, even as angels stop by for a kind of elevated well-baby check not specifically recorded in the New Testament.

What a contrast there is between the little-remembered but once robust artists' tradition of "knitting Madonnas"—with its implicit elevation of knitting as an occupation fit for God's mother—and the dismissive attitude toward knitting that has appeared in more recent art! At least the knitter in Charles Dickens' novel *A Tale of Two Cities*, Madame Defarge, is a person with strong opinions and an activist political bent. As you probably already know, however (how often people who see us knitting seem compelled to allude to her), she's a nasty, sinister figure, a vengeful French revolutionary who knits while watching people get guillotined. Jane Austen's Mrs. Bates is infinitely nicer but no more helpful for our craft's public image, a cloyingly sweet, not-very-intelligent woman who drives the novel's main character, Emma, nuts with her tiresome chatter (and will drive a reader nuts, too, thus building empathy for the complicated Emma).

Representations of knitting didn't get any more positive among twentieth century authors, when women writers championing equality used the craft as shorthand for wasted intellectual potential and defeat. Sylvia Plath described a woman knitting in winter, "her body a bulb in the cold and too dumb to think." Pioneering feminist Germaine Greer got even more direct when she termed knitting "heroic pointlessness," suggesting that it encouraged women to "fritter…their lives away."

Today the old slurs occasionally rise again, even as the contemporary knitting renaissance has made our craft wildly popular and scholars are contending that knitting really is a feminist act (if you're interested in that line of thought, see Maura Kelly's 2014 article in *Women's Studies International Forum*). Not long ago a popular actress confessed to an interviewer that although she'd once studied French and Italian, "after I had my two kids, my brain turned to mush and I took up knitting."

Given such dismissals, it may seem odd to mention "knitting" and "spirituality" in the same phrase, as this book's title does. Nevertheless the pages that follow work from the premise that those long-ago painters understood something profound, something that those of us who knit centuries later can and ought to still embrace and celebrate.

Knitting is not just a mundane, mind-numbing way to pass time we don't have better ways to fill. It is a spiritual path very much appropriate in the lives of those who sense that our world is informed by some significance beyond mere mortal physicality. Those of us who yearn to grow in understanding of mysteries beyond easy ken, and through that exploration to awaken to a deeper self-knowledge, connection, and sense of purpose, are not "frittering" our time away by knitting; we're actively taking steps on a journey toward enlightenment, reconciliation, and redemption.

The idea that knitting can be a spiritually transformative path is not original to this book, of course, as anyone familiar with knit-lit will know. Starting with Bernadette Murphy's 2002 work on knitting and Zen, a number of writers both non-theistic and conventionally religious have admirably drawn on personal experience and timeless spiritual wisdom to suggest ways that our favorite hobby can make us aware, centered, better people. So accepted has the association become that even canonical (in a literal sense) *U.S. Catholic* magazine printed an article in 2015 assuring readers that "the practice of knitting can teach a knitter a number of spiritual lessons."

This book expands on such groundwork, building on the now-familiar ideas about "lessons learned" to explore in more depth how the craft can support knitters' ongoing lifelong exploration of the mysteries within us and beyond us. Rather than mission-accomplished-style goals for the here-and-now (e.g., "knitting teaches you patience"), it deals with the never-ending, open-ended aspects of spiritual development, where each unfolding beckons you further along.

It's also different in its philosophical scope. Where many of the previous books are grounded in a particular faith or ethical system, this one is broadly cross-cultural, drawing on many wisdom traditions and on the wisdom about leading a good and worthy human life offered by secular fields including psychotherapy and educational psychology. As you read *Knitting as a Spiritual Path,* you'll meet spiritual leaders and texts both familiar and possibly new to you, philosophers and thinkers, writers and artists, famous people in the public sphere and famous knitters. You'll also encounter ordinary knitters that this writer has met over four decades of pretty much daily knitting, teaching the craft, and doing incidental pattern design around the edges of my "real life" as teacher and writer, wife and widow.

Though this book is organized into ten topics, please understand at the outset that these are not meant as discrete, isolated paths to spiritual development. While you may choose to begin to explore where you already feel comfortable or feel a need to explore, ultimately these ten ways of thinking about the spirituality of knitting are a mandala, a Sanskrit word that loosely translates to mean "circle" or "center," points of reflection that complement one another and are all necessary for full spiritual growth (as yoga's four arms of devotion, action, knowledge, self-discipline are said to do). You might think of these ten lessons as parallel tracks (or "lanes," maybe, if the roadway metaphor *really* appeals to you), all of which are going in the same direction and lead to the same ultimate end but offer different scenery on the way—and to prosper on the journey you eventually need to explore all these byways.

To make the most of this book, you might devote a day or a week or a month to each "path," using its lessons as a lens through which you pay attention to your own knitting practice, considering where it resonates and where your experience might be different and how it might be calling you to deeper consideration about some aspect of your life. Perhaps you might journal about the three questions appended to each chapter; or perhaps you'll discuss the ideas in a knitting group or with a thoughtful knitter-seeker-friend; or perhaps you'll just want to let the ideas swirl around in your own mind. In any case, if you're the sort of person who finds systematic approaches to spiritual practice congenial—who is drawn to those limbs of yoga or to St. Ignatius' spiritual exercises, for example—you're likely to feel right at home here. Even if you prefer "spontaneous knitting design" over charts as a life-strategy, however, this book offers you lots of starting points, for at its heart it's meant to be about exploration and multiplicity of experience, not a one-track guidebook on *the* right path to "do" spirituality.

As we begin, nevertheless, you do need to be aware that this book has two givens. First, it insists that the sacred and the ordinary everyday worlds are not separate spheres, that the holy interpenetrates constantly into our earthly mortal existence. In other words, it affirms that, as Lao Tzu responded when a seeker asked him how to pursue enlightenment, "Everyday life is the path." Or as Jesus prayed to his Father, "your reign come every day, on Earth as it does in Heaven." Second, it presumes that you embrace faith in the human spirit...in its goodness, its innate capacity to grow, its fundamental yearning to touch the creative mystery that encircles us and inspires our own creativity.

So integral are both of those propositions to knitting that I'll dare suggest that if you're a knitter you're almost certainly already on this spiritual path, whether you've consciously set out on it or not. Thus I offer this book in the spirit of making you more consciously aware of that journey, of facilitating and enriching the path, of inviting you daily to celebrate the wonder of this sacred human existence...not just as you ply your knitting needles but as you simultaneously shape what poet Mary Oliver called "your one wild and precious life."

Susan H. Swetman
Pocatello, Idaho
December 31, 2022
World Spirituality Day

"Let Us Assert Ourselves"
The Path of Risk and Growth

Friends know Lisa as an advanced knitter, someone practiced in many phases of the craft and not afraid to undertake the edgy experimental designs featured in high-fashion knitting magazines. ("Lisa," as with all the names for knitters featured in personal examples in the pages that follow, is a pseudonym.) Thus they're often surprised when they see her wear a particular obviously made-with-loving-hands-at-home sweater. Knit in a very basic navy worsted-weight Cascade yarn, it doesn't fit well—oversized in an "oops" way vs. a deliberate one, fitted in the shoulders and sleeves but baggy in the chest and droopy at the bottom. Its finishing is distinctly amateurish. Seeing Lisa wearing this awkward object as she knits, say, an exquisite silk lace shawl of her own design, it would be easy to assume that someone she loves made it for her, that wearing it so often is an affirmation of sentimental connection.

If you ask her about that sweater, though, you'll learn something that may make you think differently about your own history as a knitter: this is the first sweater that Lisa ever made for herself. "I love this thing," she'll admit. "Sure, it's kind of ratty compared to what I do now. But it's so comfortable—and it was my first step, ever, after garter-stitch scarves. Wearing this reminds me of how brave I was back then, thirty years ago, how I was willing to try something I was pretty sure I couldn't do. It reminds me that I can still be her, that new-knitter me, that I shouldn't ever stop stretching myself."

As you may be aware, attempting to teach an adult with no experience to knit is at once an exercise in frustration and an invitation to sudden and happy self-awareness for both the mentor and the mentee. If you've been routinely plying your needles for many years, the process of forming those stitches and keeping them where they belong will have become almost automatic; you knit while having coffee and talking with friends, while watching television or listening to an audiobook, while watching the landscape unfurl below through an airplane window—all without consciously thinking about the physical processes involved.

Working with a rookie, though, forces you to break the sequence down. Along the way, you become newly aware of the ways you've achieved your effortless competence. If you're a new teacher, you'll probably double-check your own hands before the lesson begins, refreshing your automatic-pilot memory about which direction the yarn goes around the needle, how exactly that loop is pulled through as the stitch is transferred. What you're likely to remember, but only as your student's stitches fall off the needles or as she suddenly starts knitting in the wrong direction with the object's back facing her, is how many tiny, constant micro-adjustments of the needles' position and the yarn's tension a knitter makes during the multi-step process of forming one sequential stitch at a time.

So many things can go wrong in the universe of newbies, things you'll have forgotten you once did yourself. Some first-timers, for example, attempt to improve their view of the proceedings by positioning needles with tips toward and close to their eyes rather than horizontally, to the point where "front" and "back" become confused. Some hold the working yarn so loosely that stitches slip off the needle as soon as they are formed. Others maintain such a death grip that inserting points into the second row is literally impossible. Ply splitting and stitch dropping change the stitch count in every row, prompting wails of frustration, and the new knitter's convulsive death-grip on her fabric will ensure that those dropped stitches will ladder way down...way, way down.

You, the teacher, will soon realize that it's difficult to explain how exactly to achieve these more subtle matters, because they're hard-won, touchy-feely techniques born of long experience. There's no objective standard of "pounds per inch" on yarn tension, for example—an individual knitter learns the hard way by going too far in both directions and finally memorizing the right intuitive feel. *Wow, I really know what I'm doing! It's incredible that such a complicated process has become second nature!*

So, love the student as you might, and as eager for her competence as you might be, it's easy to feel a little smug at the outset. Yet in later lessons, as her competence grows and she exclaims with joy at a new skill mastered, you might find yourself feeling just a little jealous: *It's been a long time since I felt that rush.*

If you google phrases like "adult growth and development" and "creative risk-taking," you'll find hundreds, if not thousands, of relevant links offered by a wide range of folks including business consultants, life coaches, social workers, pop psychologists, assorted gurus and pastors, and scientists studying human development.

Fortunately, if you are a knitter you don't need to spend hundreds of hours browsing to learn the truth about learning, since all these self-styled authorities say essentially the same thing: to live a fully human life is to take risks that foster exploration and personal evolution. We're innately formed as a species for growth; we are happier and healthier and more successful if we seek out risks. Risk-averse people find their relationships, their intellectual life, and their vocational and avocational development stunted as their fear of failure keeps them stuck. They're more likely to feel inadequate; they tend to become depressed and/or defensive. On the spiritual front, risk-averse people tend to gravitate to too-easy sureties and doctrinaire belief systems; their adult spirituality doesn't evolve beyond childhood simplicity. They may become self-protectively judgmental about those who believe different things than they do.

Evolution is a good thing, a necessary thing. Yet evolving isn't often easy or painless, in part because those of us who are enthusiastic about something (e.g., relationships, politics, religion, travel, etc.) often tend to bite off way more than we can chew. If you're an effective teacher of knitting—or really, anything else—you'll already know the fix for this problem: learners need logical sequencing. Students should be given the tools they need to achieve a particular level on the way to that level; the skills/risks presented must be achievable given the student's background and knowledge.

Famous, sudden, inspirational breakthroughs in spiritual awareness seem to suggest that the spiritual path operates differently from knitting (St. Paul on the road to Damascus; the future Buddha encountering a dead person; St. Pelagia the Penitent, a prostitute, who became a desert hermit after seeing an icon of the Virgin Mary). But venerable wisdom from all the world's spiritual traditions emphasizes that for most people, on most days, the one-thing-at-a-time principle holds spiritually too. Given our human nature, these traditions insist, most of us simply must approach transformation as a gradual, step-based process. To jump ahead too fast invites disillusion and setbacks (as this knitter can attest, having more than once attempted ambitious Celtic cables at a moment when she should have more properly been mastering basic twisted stitches).

Centuries-worth of spiritual masters have offered seekers progressive models of spiritual growth. Those who follow contemporary spirituality will know the excellent work of gurus like Brené Brown, Deepak Chopra, Thomas More, and Richard Rohr, but one of the wisest models is also one of the oldest, the creation of a sixteenth-century Spanish nun and mystic, Teresa of Avila. Written as instruction for Teresa's nuns and featuring the metaphor of a castle with seven rooms ("mansions") to suggest stages of the soul's journey, *The Interior Castle* (1588) begins with the seeker outside, yearning and fearful. Once the subject gathers the courage to enter the castle, she dwells first in a lowly basement room, then moves through ever-more exalted chambers, each with its own temptations and lessons. The ultimate goal is the exalted seventh room, where union with the divine beckons.

One of the great pleasures of reading *The Interior Castle* is Teresa's timeless insight into human tendencies toward self-doubt and getting stuck. Since she's writing for not-necessarily-well-educated women, she attempts to make such dangers real by framing them as "vipers and poisonous reptiles" (presumably common in that time and place). "Dare I begin this work? Would it not be presumptuous? Perhaps I shall fail," Teresa imagines a person in that scary basement saying to herself at such vipers' prompting. A few rooms above, the more subtle reptiles of "bad thoughts and aridities" periodically appear; even in the relatively advanced fourth mansion, where seekers live stable, virtuous lives of conventional piety: "Agile little lizards" may whisper that they've reached their potential and should not dare to aspire to higher mysticism.

"All things obstruct us when prudence rules our actions," Teresa sternly advises those latter readers. "Let us assert ourselves, for the love of God."

Any knitter who's ever been lured in a moment of reckless vainglory into ordering a somewhat-too-aspirational kit will be familiar with a fiber-arts species of such reptiles.

The situation goes like this. A website shows you an irresistible package deal, a nautilus-shaped open-work shawl in multi-hued, hand-painted yarn, perhaps, and you take a deep breath and push the button. When the box arrives, however, panic quickly succeeds delighted anticipation. So many colors of yarn. So many pages of instructions and elaborate, small-print charts. Should have noticed all that increasing and decreasing, all those fussy short rows. And what in the world does "yfon" mean?

It's cold comfort, but in such moments a knitter might take heart that she's already in the castle, already committed to the basic joy of knitting. The worst thing that can happen, after all, is that she may discover that she's not yet ready to move up to the next mansion and put the kit aside or give it to someone else. At least she's not one of those pre-rookies lingering in the courtyard outside the castle, thinking it would be kind of cool to be a knitter, even as they contend with the tangle of preliminary vipers swirling at their feet. Just making the decision to buy that kit—unfortunate as the act might have been in the short term—proves that in the long-term the knitter is a risk-taker, a person yearning to grow, committed to evolving from that basement of garter-stitch washcloths to the mansions of lace and Aran and colorwork, or perhaps eventually to the sixth room where Lisa, wearing her learner sweater, is knitting whatever that weird asymmetrical mix-tape drapey thing is.

Here's to learning and to teaching. Here's to honoring—in small things as in big—the love that has created us as beings so full of potential.

Questions for Reflection or Discussion

1. Were you ever "stuck" in your knitting, or your life? What happened, why do you think that happened, and how did you break out of it? What risks might you take as a knitter to stretch yourself even more?

2. Imagine both small steps and dream projects that would invite you to take risks as you explore your capacity.
3. Are you bored with or too complacent about any aspect of your life right now? How might you reframe the situation to challenge yourself in healthy, growth-promoting ways? How might your knitting help you get there?

Knitting Alone

The Path of Stillness

Victorian "lady traveler" Isabella Bird was a person of seemingly boundless energy, courage, and optimism—a woman whose life challenged the gender stereotypes of her late nineteenth-century British culture. Though fragile and ill in youth, once Bird discovered the pleasures of travel (recommended by her doctor to improve her health) she became a vigorous world explorer. A celebrated writer (author of eight books and many articles), naturalist, and photographer, she was the first woman ever elected to the United Kingdom's prestigious national academy of sciences, the Royal Society. Bird was a bold and excellent horsewoman, who usually traveled with a guide but sometimes absolutely alone, and the roster of wild, strange, and dangerous places she visited still holds the power to amaze: India, Kurdistan, Tibet, Japan, Morocco, Hawaii, Persia, the Yangtze and Han rivers in China and Korea.

One of the few occasions when Bird admitted in print to being downcast happened, though, not in one of the wildest corners of the world but in Colorado—a place already settled by English-speaking people long before she arrived in 1873, though admittedly remote by the standards of the British countryside. As chronicled in her book, *A Lady's Life in the Rocky Mountains*, the fraught moment came as landscape-loving Bird attempted to reach the celebrated beauty spot of Estes Park, then an unspoiled gateway to the high Rockies. She realized, however, that she would be forced to stay for several days at a slovenly boarding house in the foothills run by rough,

ill-humored people while she waited for a competent guide and a horse. When the buggy that had delivered her to the compound had disappeared and the intrepid traveler inspected the tiny cabin where she'd sleep (visited by small wild animals who came in through its chinks), even this bold soul confessed that as a woman traveling alone she felt for a moment completely abandoned and frightened.

Quickly, though, Bird regained her composure thanks to a simple strategy whose effectiveness she'd long trusted. "I sat down and knitted," she tells her readers, "my usual recourse under discouraging circumstances."

Just about every knitter—fumbling beginners aside perhaps—will know exactly the sort of knitting-induced calm Isabelle Bird is describing. Indeed, a calm and reflective state of mind has long been recognized as a hallmark of the craft, a phenomenon described in fiction, non-fiction, and personal essays in women's and knitting magazines, and discussed informally as an incontrovertible truth among knitters.

"You see? Now you're acting like knitters," this writer once heard a knitting teacher in Iceland affirm, smiling as her mixed-nationality class went peacefully silent over the challenging stranded slippers they'd been complaining about a few minutes before. "You're going to be just fine."

Thanks to the renaissance of craft that has brought knitting newly to researchers' attention in recent years, this calming effect has been clearly, objectively documented and its causes deeply examined. For example, Harvard scientists found in 2007 that knitters' heart rates decreased by an average of eleven beats per minute; their blood pressure also went down to more healthy levels after just a short interval of focused knitting. Other peer-reviewed studies discovered that the repetitive motions of knitting encouraged practitioners' brains to release feel-good natural chemicals, including serotonin, and to inhibit the production of fight-or-flight stress hormones.

The bilateral (two-handed) nature of the craft has been hypothesized to gently stimulate neurons all over the brain, thus promoting brain health. Whatever the physiological mechanism, a 2011 Mayo Clinic study suggested a substantial link between knitting and retaining brain-power: among a large sample population of elderly people studied over time, those who knit were 30-50% less likely than the others to suffer mild cognitive decline. Elderly people who knit are also more likely to sleep better, according to a journal concerned with nursing home administration, which documented the efficacy of knitting as a form of "self-hypnosis" in treating insomnia.

Iconic British knitting designer/teacher/writer Elizabeth Zimmerman, a tireless innovator (especially in her advocacy of circular knitting) and someone who brought a meticulously detailed and disciplined approach to design (through her mathematical "percentage system" of sweater construction), was no stranger to the calm that knitting can bring. "Properly practiced, knitting soothes the troubled spirit," one of her most-quoted remarks goes. "And it doesn't hurt the untroubled spirit either."

Zimmerman's use of "spirit" (instead of, say, "mind" or "person") is telling in the context of this book, since "soothing the troubled spirit" (or "soul") is something that most if not all religious practice—whether prayer or song or reading scripture—is widely purported to be able to do. A recent writer on knitting, Peggy Rosenthal, explicitly fuses knitting and soul-soothing in her book, *Knit One, Purl a Prayer,* the latter phrase coming from an introductory story about a woman knitting an afghan for her troubled runaway daughter and calming her own fears in the process.

No less a spiritual model than Dorothy Day—the twentieth-century American social-justice advocate who has reached the "Blessed" stage on her path to Catholic sainthood (and who knew something about having a "troubled spirit," according to the recent biography by her granddaughter, Kate Hennessy, *Dorothy Day: The World Will Be Saved by Beauty*)—also associated knitting with spiritual practice. Day was an inveterate knitter throughout her life, making useful items for the poor and her extended "family" at the series of Catholic Worker settlement houses she founded in New York and elsewhere and on cooperatively-run farms in the countryside. Day knitted while with her biological family or on personal retreats, knitted as she traveled to give talks and raise funds. Knitting, she once affirmed, was a particular blessing in her work as a writer, whether for her own journal, *The Catholic Worker,* the many other magazines in which she published, or her autobiography, *The Long Loneliness*. As knitting quieted her, she suggested, it also opened her mind to inspiration. "Knitting is very conducive to thought," she said. "It is nice to knit for a while, put down the needles, write for a while, then take up the sock again."

Retreating from the world's busy-ness for a time to calm the mind, as Day did, has for thousands of years been held to promote spiritual experiences including holy insight, a feeling of beneficent connection with others, and intimation of forces beyond our rational ken. When a person is centered and calm in meditation, spiritual teacher Thich Nhat Hanh once said, "you touch the miracle of being alive . . . touch the wonder of life, in you and around you."

Perhaps the best-known spiritual practice in the context of the specific word "meditation" is the "sitting" central to Buddhism. Recommended as a daily discipline, sitting involves calmly resting and focusing on the breath, perhaps repeating a mantra (a sacred word or phrase). Those who sit seek to quiet the "monkey mind"—the tendency our brains have to be nervous and flighty as we obsess about the future or past, judge ourselves or others, and become distracted by things in the immediate environment or out in "the world."

In recent decades some Christians have adopted that sitting practice into "contemplative prayer" (advocated by Thomas Keating, OCSO, among others), where the meditator repeats a specifically Christian word or phrase as a mantra. Yet meditation in the broader sense (to engage in reflection) and in the particular sense described above (of sitting in receptive stillness) has been in actuality a feature of Christianity for many centuries, especially prominent in monastic life, in particular, since the Middle Ages. Many nuns, monks, and spiritual teachers, including the ascetic desert hermits, Gertrude the Great, Hildegard of Bingen, Julian of Norwich, John of the Cross, Teresa of Ávila, Meister Eckhart, and Thomas Merton have found that quieting their minds could provide a profound experience of infinite divine presence.

In varied ways, but with the same aim of religious enlightenment through quieting the rational mind, Jews, Muslims, Buddhists, Taoists, and Confucians meditate. Hindus and Sikhs also meditate, and one of their practices, the musical genre called *Kirtan,* might appeal to you if you're a knitter who likes to listen to music as you work. This writer, anyway, has found this lovely repetitive call-and-response form—with its evocation of an ordered cosmos—to elevate my knitting-induced calm into a decidedly "religious experience."

You don't even have to subscribe to a particular doctrinal or philosophical system to meditate, as the current popularity of the mind-body movement attests. People uneasy with traditional denominationalism or individual ethical systems can tap into guidance on generic meditation via popular magazines (e.g., *Spirituality and Health*), through books by best-selling spiritual writers (e.g., Alan Watts, Sadhguru), and through institutions that offer meditation classes and retreats that welcome those of any persuasion, or none at all (e.g., Sivananda ashrams, Esolen). Every day in this country, in communities of any size, agnostics and outright atheists practice non-religious yoga alongside those who hold more conventional religious beliefs, seeking serenity as well as physical, psychological, and emotional health.

Same with knitters. We are a diverse group of human beings, young and old, with a variety of family and personal situations, gender identities, political views, and religious beliefs. And all we have to do to access the focused quiet that invites insight, peace, and connection is to pick up our needles.

Questions for Reflection or Discussion

1. Describe one time knitting calmed you in a time of particular personal anxiety or stress. Have you ever enjoyed s moment of spontaneous insight or problem-solving while knitting? If so, tell that story.
2. Do you engage in other forms of meditation? If so, have you combined them with your knitting? If so, what happened? If not, what other discipline might you like to explore as you knit?

3. How might you make more space for the centering, spirit-enhancing benefits of contemplation? Be specific. Put contemplation (including while knitting) into your weekly appointment calendar, and when it pops up, try it right then and there for whatever time you have. (If you can't, then simply move the "appointment" to another time or day.)

Knitting with Others
The Path of Fellowship

The knitting group meets like clockwork every weekend. On occasion, its fifteen-or-so participants will agree to focus on knitting for charity (recently they made hats for the needy), but for most sessions each knitter brings an item suitable for simultaneous work and conversation: i.e., nothing too complicated. They gather in the homey back space of a coffee shop happy to host them (prodigious quantities of coffee and pastries are purchased and consumed), and the women knit and get caught up with one another for about two hours.

Fiction about knitting groups suggests that profoundly moving and exciting things happen constantly at such gatherings. Participants help each other through the major crises of their lives (cancer, widowhood, the death of a child); they confess addiction or depression or adultery; they work through deep jealousies and conflicts among themselves; they solve murder mysteries. In this group, though, the talk is consistently unremarkable: members report the doings of grandchildren, the antics of pets, the ordinary domestic frustrations (a broken dishwasher, a repairman who blew off an appointment). They share news of vacations and remodeling. The ones who are employed might share a little of their success or frustration at work; the ones who are married will tell something funny their spouse did. To an outsider, the whole business might seem incredibly mundane, even tedious.

Yet group members' posts on social media suggest these quiet gatherings provide sisterhood that anchors their weeks.

Perhaps it is no accident, after all, that this particular knitting circle gathers on Sunday mornings.

Knitters whose travels take them to unfamiliar cities or who have recently relocated to one place or another on the globe have many happy options these days for finding like-minded new friends. Most yarn shops host gatherings at least one night a week and, if you happen to be looking for a different day, staff members and shop bulletin boards will point you to other groups in the vicinity. In fact, you often don't even need an organized group; in many stores you'll be invited to sit at a table in the midst of the yarn and knit if you feel like it, visiting as you like or not with other drop-ins.

Finding new knitting friends can also be initiated online by simply googling "knitting groups near me." Don't believe me? Try it. What you'll find is riches indeed—an array of possibilities that drives home just how popular our craft has become. The Knitting Circle page on meetup.com, for example, is especially notable for its amplitude, documenting 328 groups and 74,925 members across the world. It's nice to know that if you ever find yourself with yarn and time on your hands in, say, Burnaby, British Columbia; or Abuja, Nigeria; or London or Bath; or just about any place where your car might need an overnight repair or a plane might be grounded by bad weather, there are new knitting friends interested in meeting you. You can also just enter a community name and "knitting" on Facebook, and you'll be hooked up with the locals in communities both large (Chicago's Knit and Crochet group) and small (Idaho's Pocatello Knitters).

So, unless you're way out in the absolute middle of nowhere or in one of the few benighted places still untouched by the knitting revival, there's pretty much no reason for you to ply your lonely needles in a hotel room or empty new house, unless you want to, of course.

It's easy to understand why knitting groups are so popular. Most basically, human beings are "social animals," as the cliché goes, and therefore we naturally enjoy company and conversation. There are also more craft-specific reasons for the Camaraderie of Yarn: every knitter knows she can sometimes use a little expert advice, and chances are that someone in just about any knitting circle can remind you how to do the Kinschner Stitch sequence or help you diagnose just what has gone wrong with the botched crossings in that now-chaotic cable you're working on. Besides, any good knitter uses the inspiration of others' work for an unexpected color combination or a cool way to hack a collar design to hide a little more of a wrinkly neck.

Social contact can also be had online or over the phone, though, and many really good lessons can be learned on YouTube or Ravelry. But the in-person human contact, obviously, is the biggest attraction of knitting together. It's certainly the one that has been most discussed by bloggers and commentators, professional sociologists and psychologists who study the effects of hobbies. Their universal deduction is hardly revolutionary: people are especially drawn to knitting (and other) groups in this twenty-first century because loneliness is endemic in our culture. And the problem is getting worse in the polarized, contentious world we've managed to build for ourselves. (Not the knitters, mind you. We're perfectly happy to just sit and knit. But everyone else!)

Nothing quite substitutes for others' physical attentive presence, observers remind us, and we're getting less and less of that presence all the time. We humans now entertain ourselves by hunching over isolated computers rather than gathering together. We work so many hours at our jobs that we're too exhausted for socializing. More and more of us every year are living alone. The number of adults in single-person households has nearly doubled in the past fifty years.

As our world "feels lonelier than ever" (to quote a 2016 British Mental Health Foundation report), we become vulnerable to anxiety and depression. Extremely isolated people might suffer Depersonalization Syndrome, feeling unreal and dislocated from their bodies. Even with mild anxiety, though, a vicious circle can follow. The more down a person feels, the more anxious she becomes about socializing, fearing that she will not know what to say or how to act or fearing she will have nothing in common with the others in the group and nothing to contribute and thus be harshly judged.

That's where knitting groups come in. There will *always* be something in common to talk about at one of these gatherings (duh, knitting!), and when you speak there will be no pressure to be a constantly-brilliant conversationalist or to feel obliged to fill up awkward silences—the ostensible purpose of the circle is handwork, not entertaining each other with *bon mots*. It is implicitly (and sometimes explicitly) understood that periodically silence will fall upon a group of knitters (see chapter one).

And if you're really shy, you can keep your gaze on your work instead of making eye contact. It's pretty much guaranteed that in every meeting of knitters there will be a lot of companionable laughter and encouragement, the latter extended especially toward beginners.

Thus it's no surprise that research on knitting groups suggests that such participation significantly boosts group members' perceived happiness level and their sense of meaningful social connection. "Since I joined the knitting group," one respondent told an interviewer, "I have a deeper sense of mattering to somebody. Before, I felt like if I died nobody would notice."

Becca, the woman who established the coffee-shop knitting group described at the start of this chapter, is herself an exemplar of the happiness and healing that knitting with others can afford. Today an outgoing, bright-faced woman with almost more friends than she knows what to do with, Becca found herself fifteen years ago at an extremely low point in her life. The consequences of growing up in a dysfunctional religious-fundamentalist family—reminiscent in some respects of the one Tara Westover describes in the novel *Educated*—had finally caught up with Becca, and despite all the efforts of a loving husband she found herself (as she has spoken about publicly in various knitting forums) in mental breakdown.

Becca's disability forced her to resign from her career as a counselor for college students; she was hospitalized several times as doctors struggled to find the right combination of medications. She felt like she'd let everyone down, like there was no reason to go on living.

Becca was starting to think that things would never get better. Then, at the recommendation of a therapist familiar with the concept that knitting could quiet troubled minds, she found herself walking into a yarn store. She had never even tried to knit, but the owners and several of Becca's acquaintances were glad to provide instruction and encouragement. Before long, as an alternative to sitting alone and frightened at home, Becca summoned all her courage and joined the informal drop-in afternoon knitting circle at the store. Everybody was delighted to get to know this sweet soul, and Becca's superb listening skills quickly made her a favorite. Before long she was instructing and encouraging others.

When the store's owners announced that they would be retiring and the store closing, many mourned in anticipation. Becca, in contrast, took the steps to ensure that the group would continue. She held initial meetings in her own house, then convinced public venues like that coffeeshop and the local library to host. In the subsequent years, she's made knitting prominent and inclusive in our town, building a community where anyone who could use some companionship and connection can feel at home. She runs learn-to-knit classes for troubled teenagers and at-risk adults. The knitting circles she's organized are notably diverse and community-building, including people who are living on the economic margins as well as hospital administrators and university professors. Housewives, teenagers, and young adults mingle with elderly and handicapped people.

Becca also organizes special events like knitting camp-outs in the nearby national forest and communal trips to regional destination yarn stores and festivals. She established a website that currently boasts 190 members and finds herself the vastly-admired, deeply-loved linchpin of our thriving, righteous community.

It's a measure of how important the knitting has become to participants that, even in the midst of Covid-19 social isolation, these knitters were still inventing ways to reach one another. Zoom "knit-alongs" happened regularly; web-group members posted more pictures than ever of their projects and exclaimed over those of others. Feelers were extended and accepted for "knit-in-the-park" sessions where participants sat a decorous six feet apart. "I MISS everybody so much, can't WAIT to do this," one of Becca's knitters posted online, a sentiment often repeated.

"Walk in the light...of fellowship with one another," "bear each other's burdens," Paul urged groups of early Christians (1 John 1:7; Gal 6:2), emphasizing that the lives of those awakened to truth ought to reflect the divine compassion that cradles all creation. Constructing fellowship, as Paul frames it, is nothing less than a sacred practice, one in which human conduct affirms the holy fact that our lives are inseparably interconnected, that being spiritual people obliges us to look out for one another.

Because of the changes in our society, though, such practice today takes place most often not in obviously religious contexts but in modest interactions you might discount if you didn't know how or where to look. Peace flourishes in quiet moments spent in others' company, in gatherings that bear a silent but unmistakable witness: *You are someone I want to spend my time with; you are worthy, known, and loved.*

In the ordinary fellowship of knitting circles, for example.

Questions for Reflection or Discussion

1. How would you define sisterhood and fellowship? Do you agree that building and sustaining relationships can be "a sacred practice?" In what respects? Give some examples from your own life or that of others you have observed.
2. Has your participation in knitting or any other kind of intentional groups impacted your sense of community? How specifically? Why do you think this happened?
3. Do you know someone who needs a deeper sense of belonging? Brainstorm ways you might reach out to him/her, with or without knitting needles.

Knitting in Public

The Path of Equanimity

"I used to be an off-again, on-again knitter," Denita admits when a member of her knitting group remarks on how quickly she completes projects. "I'd go weeks without picking up the needles; it took me forever to finish anything."

She shakes her head, remembering. "But that sure changed the year I was acting dean at the university while they were looking for somebody permanent. When I agreed I knew there'd be lots of hard work cleaning up the mess the guy who'd just left had made, but I was actually looking forward to doing it. What I didn't anticipate was all the meetings I'd have to sit through: deans' council meetings, university provost's and president's weekly staff meetings, state board of education meetings. Sure, some important things happened, but people got so mad at each other, really nasty, not listening to one another, getting on high horses, bullying. And there was so much wasted time—people just talked on and on, repeating, posturing, saying things that were just ridiculous. I watched myself get grumpier and grumpier and realized, *I'm going to blow up before long.*"

Then one morning, Denita had a revelation. "'Would you mind if I brought my knitting?' I asked the people in charge, and they all smiled and said I could, and everything was different from then on. I actually started looking forward to meetings because they gave me a good knitting block of time. Even when we were already over time I'd be, like, 'keep talking for another five minutes, keep the meeting going until I finish this row.' Everyone would smile or laugh and it was great—calmed me down so I could be a lot more effective, instead of getting all riled up with everybody else. The most upset I ever got after that was the day I sat down and realized I'd forgotten to bring my project bag and had a little panic attack. Looking back, I think knitting saved my life that year…and maybe some other people's."

Someone in the knitting circle asks if she wasn't afraid that the men in those meetings would stereotype her as a "little woman" because she plied this oh-so-domestic art in public.

"Nope," Denita says. "I figured what I said at the meetings and how I said it would take care of that." She waves her hand airily. "And I was in good company. Eleanor Roosevelt used to knit in meetings, and even at the United Nations and in Congress, after all. Nobody ever 'little-womaned' her. She inspired me to make sure nobody did that to me, either."

"Virtue isn't virtue until it's tested," a common aphorism goes, and any knitter who ventures out from the peace of solitary craft or a congenial knitting group to knit out in the world will inevitably find that truth driven home. It's relatively easy to be still and composed and caring in situations where little stress exists, after all, and we might be tempted to become a little smug, congratulating ourselves on being islands of peace in a sadly anxious and often tension-filled world. When we are obliged to re-enter that world, however—whether into meetings like Denita's or into other contexts pulsing with potential stress—knitting-induced virtue is very likely to be shaken.

Let's face it: the vast majority of us human beings are anything but serene. Even the briefest look at the news (or driving on a highway at rush hour) will demonstrate just how prevalent self-centeredness, competition, and pure nastiness are in our species' behavior (often including our own).

Why, if theologically or philosophically we believe people are supposed to be good most of the time, are we in the mess we are in today? Evolutionary biologists say that competition for resources, survival, and even sexual or soul mates has been built into our DNA from our days in the savannahs. Karl Marx argued that capitalism intensified that problem by forcing people to contend for their share of limited resources. The conventional wisdom of modern secular society urges us to look out for ourselves and our own. If you move too slowly, the assumption is, you're going to be run over. If you show any sign of compromise or giving in, you're going to be taken for a ride. If things don't go your way, you're a pathetic failure. "I like winners," one of our recent Presidents proclaimed.

Competition and entitlement are contagious. If you've ever had a flight canceled and were directed to sit and wait in the boarding area to be called up individually to rebook, that certainly doesn't have to be pointed out to you. All it takes is one person crowding up to the desk out of turn, shoving, demanding, for everybody to be tempted to do the same. If you've gone to a meeting with the intention of listening with the common good in mind, when others begin aggressively advocating for their points of view it's difficult to hold off on joining in to protect your side.

It doesn't even take someone else's bad behavior to trigger ours; we're also perfectly capable of self-generating aggressive anxiety, thanks to the monkey-mind syndrome I mentioned in chapter two. Just having to sit and wait longer than you'd like for something—a customer-service representative to answer your call, a train or a friend that's running late, the results of a medical procedure—can trigger a troubled spirit. You know the feeling: the unpleasant physical rush of adrenaline, the clenched hands, the slightly upset stomach, the urge to check your text messages or emails.

Escalation of fight-or-flight hormones, whether internally or externally sparked, obviously isn't good for you or for anybody else. But it's also not helpful for the progress of collective humanity toward a mutually-beneficial situation in the present moment, much less the evolution of our species toward third-millennial enlightenment.

Yet, as Denita's experience suggests, we knitters are uniquely positioned on a very localized level to at least try to disrupt this dire cycle—as long as we remember to bring our knitting bags to all potentially stressful situations! For while there's no guarantee that we will be able to defuse others' competitive self-serving impulses, we *can* mitigate our own responses as we extend personal serenity into public equanimity.

"Equanimity"—the ability to stay balanced and centered in the face of potential stressors, to discipline knee-jerk emotions, and to focus on the big picture—has long been considered a hallmark of laudable citizens of the human race. Roman Stoics (including the emperor Marcus Aurelius) went so far as to consider this "evenness of mind" (from the Latin root *aequanimitatem*) a necessity for anyone who wished to live a contented, productive, exemplary life.

The world's great religions join in counseling such higher self-control: *samatvam* in Hinduism, *upeksa* in Buddhism, *menuhat ha-nefesh* or *yishuv ha-da'at* in Judaism. Medieval Christians included *equanimity* as one of the seven cardinal virtues, naming it *temperance,* a term it still bears in the Tarot deck, where drawing the card with this designation is said to counsel synthesis, harmony, and win-win problem solving.

To knit in public is to pursue this virtue, whether deliberately or not. All those innately calming physical aspects of knitting I described in chapter two predispose us to slow down, which in turn helps us listen to others' perspectives and pay attention to our own inner dialogue with greater attention.

Also, a person such as Denita who knits in stressful interpersonal situations imposes upon herself a healthy mandatory lag-time relative to shooting from the hip. She needs to finish the stitch, at least, and arrange the needles so the row doesn't go rogue before she responds to someone else's outrageous statement—and that instant can offer enough time to catch herself before she says something she'll regret.

More subjectively, knitting also physically reminds its practitioner that the present moment is just a fleeting one in the larger scheme of life. Even as a knitter endures a localized tempest in a teapot, after all, she's still holding a little piece of connection to the "larger world" on her lap, an artifact glowing with happy reminders of inception and future that have absolutely nothing to do with this moment.

And then there's that "keep talking till I finish this row" phenomenon that Denita experienced. Any "found" knitting time is necessarily going to make the knitting enthusiast happy, and that will make otherwise tedious moments much easier to bear. Everybody else might be miserable, running out of patience and wanting a meeting or event to be over now. But the knitters in the room? At least part of their mind is having fun, and that's going to make them more pleasant, patient, and easier to get along with. If you don't believe me, you're just going to have to test it on yourself.

Denita's knitting-spirituality role model, Eleanor Roosevelt, was all-too-familiar with stressful situations, yet she managed to cultivate the equanimity essential for doing an immense amount of good. As a tireless advocate for human rights, the wife of President Franklin Delano Roosevelt endured rancorous, sometimes unseemly verbal smears in print (the far-right newspaper columnist Westbrook Pegler routinely called her *La Boca Grande,* "The Big Mouth"). Ignoring such slurs rather than engaging in back-and-forth, Roosevelt retained her focus on what mattered: civil rights and women's issues; the admittance of refugees before, during, and after World War II; and—let's applaud it—world peace.

Roosevelt fostered progress through regular radio shows and a weekly syndicated newspaper column; she attended Congress, sitting in the gallery as she gathered material for her remarks. In her later years she became America's first official representative at the United Nations, serving as the chair of its Commission on Human Rights. She also chaired John F. Kennedy's Presidential Commission on the Status of Women.

Through it all, Roosevelt knit as she traveled from one responsibility to another, and people took lots and lots of pictures of her knitting. Those of us who are knitters understand Eleanor's knitting wasn't just a sign of her down-to-earth, no-idle-hands philosophy of life (though it did reflect that), but it also must have helped her manage her moods, including frustration, anger, and boredom. Her knitting-induced composure must have gone a long way toward allowing her to move with effectively detached grace through the flying mud, the contentious or dull meetings, the times when she would rather have been doing something else. Without knitting, it might have been a good deal harder for Roosevelt to become "the first lady of the world," as Harry S. Truman called her. "It isn't enough to talk about peace," Roosevelt once said. "One must believe in it. And it isn't enough to believe in it. One must work at it."

Though the public peace we knitters seek today may be decidedly less global than Roosevelt's, it's good to remember that we, too, "work at it" every time we stitch as she did, through whatever tempting din surrounds us. Every time we do, we publicly, but usually silently, proclaim equanimity, hoping that it might rub off—at least a little or at least for a little while—on those around us.

Questions for Reflection or Discussion

1. What public situations habitually inspire stress for you? Recount a time when you or someone you observed used knitting to avoid getting sucked into aggressive,

non-productive, competitive, and self-centered behavior. How do you feel about what happened? Or could happen?

2. Brainstorm three strategies you might use to maintain equanimity in such contexts. Do or could you knit in such situations, and does/might that help? Why or why not?
3. Do you believe that knitters are by nature more prone to equanimity than others? That they often can or do help defuse anxiety in others? Why do you think this is so? Explain your answer with examples.

Knitting Gifts for Other People

The Path of Persistent Love

The socks are about 1,000 years old, held in the collection of London's Victoria and Albert Museum. Egyptian in origin, they're widely considered to be the oldest example of true knitting. If you're an aficionado of sock knitting, they'll look odd to you: their outline is wide and squat (can legs have been that big around and short in those days?); they lack the calf shaping that helps modern socks stay up; they're made of cotton (wool was used in knitting only in later centuries) and appear to be coarse and scratchy, a far cry from the cozy socks we produce today from soft fingering-weight yarn, whether top-down or bottom-up.

Yet these small garments speak eloquently of continuity in our craft. They testify that from its roots knitting wasn't about just utility but about delight in creativity and beauty. For despite their blocky dimensions, these socks are elegantly decorated. Geometric designs on them form dark patterning on a light background, reminiscent of Norwegian or Salishan style, colorwork that would have required attention and pattern memory. The ancient knitter who created them has obviously taken extra time with these socks, ensuring that the recipient would feel adorned and special, not just warm.

And there's an even more explicit testimony to the caring connection between the maker and the wearer of these venerable socks: within that geometric pattern are Arabic characters signifying a blessing.

Though we'll never know the identity of this ancient knitter, anyone who knits a millennium later will recognize that person as a kindred spirit to the knitters of our century. We knitters today may not include literal spiritual text in our designs, but nevertheless our knitted gifts embody a kind of blessing, making tangible our wishes for the recipient's warmth, comfort, and confident adornment. Now as then, to knit a gift is an act that cultivates active love for another person.

So many steps in the process of constructing a garment (or a pillow, or even a potholder) require the knitter to review with loving attention what is known about the recipient's needs and preferences. Sometimes surreptitious research or observation is required, and we grow in knowledge of the other. (Ever peeked at the size label in a sweater draped over the back of a chair? Ever made careful note of the exact shade of a winter jacket in a closet to make sure you match the scarf you're planning as a winter gift?).

How the gift will be worn or used dictates yarn and pattern selection—will this recipient have lots of occasions to use a lacy light-weight sweater in a pastel color, or is she more of a worsted weight natural-color outdoorsy type? What cut will look best on his or her body type, and can the pattern be modified for length of body or sleeves for a perfect fit on that basketball player? Can the pattern be converted from a crewneck to the turtleneck or v-neck style she prefers? Is he allergic to wool? Will the recipient be willing to commit to hand-washing or dry-cleaning for silk or cashmere's luxury, or is it better to use yarn that does not shrink in the washer/dryer?

In the case of household objects, what's the color scheme of that kitchen or living room the piece is intended for? Is its style country-cute or modern minimalist? To get those things wrong is to defeat one of the core pleasures of giving and receiving a handmade gift: the heart-filling assurance of *I know you.*

During the actual knitting process, many triggers invite us also to imagine future scenes involving the person. We smile to anticipate the gift's opening, dreaming of a moment of wonder and grateful tears. "That's perfect!" we fantasize hearing. "How did you know I needed that?" We project into the farther future, too, imagining the recipient wearing or using the gift during a daily routine or festive situation, getting compliments, and announcing, "My wife (mother, daughter, niece, friend) knitted this for me." We hope that the recipient of our love's fruit will feel more self-confident, and we dare to fancy (let's admit it) that we'll be held consciously in his or her heart whenever it is employed.

The time we invest in that gift's making also helps us practice love by inviting self-sacrifice. As we work, we're necessarily putting on hold other things we could be doing (including knitting for ourselves), spending our leisure in the interest of making someone else happy. On occasion, as when a holiday, a wedding or graduation or birthday, or a baby's birth is looming, we might even sacrifice our sleep, rising before dawn and staying up late to ensure that the gift is completed on time.

When the object is finished and presented and exclaimed over, all that time and labor will seem worthwhile (unless the receiver's off-handed response proves her to be non-knit-worthy, and in that case at least we've at least learned something useful about where to lodge our affections). Recipients who are true friends will wear or display the thing in our presence even if they don't absolutely love it. They may offer social media posts of it in use, tagging us and thanking us in public, and as likes and comments accumulate the labor will seem to have been light, indeed.

The process of knitting gifts, admittedly, doesn't inevitably play out in this lovely way, as your own knitting history may have demonstrated. Occasionally the process of constructing something for a friend lasts longer than the friendship, and the partially-finished object becomes a poignant, even tragic reminder of disconnection rather than an affirmation of love. Knitting folklore abounds with stories about mid-project romantic break-ups—a beau's half-finished sweater tossed from a cliff into the sea or burned in a bonfire or thrown out with the most redolent garbage in a ritual designed both to vent rage and to promote an absolute, healthy break. In a variation on this scenario, a twenty-something knitter of this writer's acquaintance found another, more constructive way to cancel out the past when her boyfriend dumped her mid-way through a complicated cabled vest. Instead of obliterating all trace of the garment, she matter-of-factly unraveled it and stowed the yarn away, neatly balled with pattern and needles, in a zippered bag in her closet. "Somebody else will come along," this healthy optimist assured us all. And somebody else did before too long, and the vest was reconstructed and delivered in a slightly different size to her delighted new boyfriend without a whisper about its backstory (except for now).

More emotionally complicated—and infinitely more common—are the situations where a relationship becomes temporarily strained but does not break during a gift's construction. "So there I was sitting on the couch the other night, and Jamal was across the room reading, and we've just had this big argument and we're not talking to each other." Jocelyn made a wry face as she confessed over coffee. "And suddenly it strikes me. I'm so mad at my husband, I kind of want to kill him! I just had a fantasy about going away somewhere by myself for the weekend—hell, maybe the rest of the month. But what am I doing? I'm sitting there spending my evening working on *his* sweater! It was so ridiculous!"

Jocelyn shook her head, remembering. "Then I thought to myself—*Guess you're not so absolutely fed up with him as you thought you were!*"

I returned her smile, remembering a period not long before when I'd continued to pour intense effort into a lace scarf for a friend with whom I was out of sorts, and another occasion when a friend I knew was angry with me showed up at my door after a long interval of separation with a sweet peace offering of a pair of warm mittens in my favorite color.

"Love is patient, love is kind...it does not brood over injury... it bears all things, believes all things, hopes all things, endures all things." I Corinthians 13:4-7 sets an ideal that can seem unattainable. Yet every knitter who persists in completing a project in the context of a strained relationship is affirming her fidelity to that standard, for to persevere in such circumstances is tacitly to manifest the belief that the power of love will be strong enough to weather the storm.

Yes, in extreme cases such stubborn persistence can reflect self-destructive denial or misguided wishful thinking; not all rifts are capable of being or even should be repaired. Yet if the situation is not so cut and dried, knitting for a distanced one is a most healthy activity, indicating a nuanced and mature understanding of what it means to love and be loved. "Being married and being a friend are active verbs," a wise man the writer once knew used to say. "Love is hard work," he would insist, "and you need to be willing to recommit to it every day. You can't prevent disagreements and wrangles from coming up—that's just the nature of human relationships. But if you really love and want to be loved, you need to cultivate the active, deliberate habit of seeing beyond temporary problems to the long term."

Ridiculously knitting on after a falling out, you might say, represents a stellar embodiment of that long-term view, a shining affirmation of that biblical standard for love.

"It's fun," I assured the earnest woman who'd marveled at how "incredibly generous" I was to use my time waiting in the doctor's office to knit a gift. I love knitting, I told her, and this gave me a chance to make something different. The effort wasn't a sacrifice—it was a pleasure.

And yet, as I must confess and I bet you might be able to also, occasionally circumstances can indeed make this business of twining yarn into fabric for someone else feel like a decided chore.

If you've been knitting for long, you're likely to have a story like this: you didn't happen to notice, say, that you were going to be casting on 325 circular fingering-weight stitches and working up from the bottom for thirteen inches before the interesting colorwork started on that Christmas sweater. Or you committed yourself to lacework that had to be done on both right and wrong sides on that graduation scarf. It would have been so easy to quit; but you'd already spilled the anticipatory beans and the recipient was so looking forward to the thing. Thus you persisted, practicing needle-style "endurance," as Corinthians advises, disciplining yourself in the name of love.

The most purely selfless knitting is certainly the practice of creating gifts for charitable causes. In this case there's no direct reward to anticipate. You'll never see the happy smile on the face of the hospitalized child or veteran who receives your blanket, the homeless one who wraps a cold neck in your scarf, or the breast cancer survivor who gratefully employs your "knitted knockers" (this is a wonderful cause, by the way, and if you're not aware of it you should be). Yet nearly all knitters fabricate such gifts from their talent, treasure, and time.

"May you know peace; may you have freedom from fear, may you know love," Buddhist practitioners of loving-kindness meditation intone for friends, strangers, even enemies; and they believe they gain great spiritual merit by that proclamation.

We knitters might not say such words aloud, but as we shape yarn-formed wishes for healing, peace, and blessings for those we cherish and for those we'll never meet, we can rest in the knowledge that we're walking exactly that same path, incarnating love in the gifts we create.

Questions for Reflection or Discussion

1. Think about the process you go through when you're knitting a gift for someone. Describes three ways in which the process invites you to practice love.
2. Has knitting ever helped make a friendship or heal one for you? Remember and/or tell someone the story in detail.
3. List other ways besides knitting you bless others through your actions or thoughts. Now add knitting to the list and prioritize which of the actions you feel are most efficacious for you and others. Where does knitting come in? Why?

Knitters Are Rippers

The Path of Humility and Imperfection

"I should have known better than to be knitting two-color brioche in the car when I was tired and the light was fading." Carrie raised her hands, palms up, in a gesture that expressed something like *how dumb was that?* "But I hadn't had much time to knit for the past three days on the trip—we'd been sightseeing in the daytime, and after dinner we'd been playing board games in the vacation rental—and I was craving just another half-hour or so on the way home, just till it got real dark." Soon she noticed that she'd made an obvious mistake

in the previous row of her pattern, and when she tried to go back so she could correct the problem she dropped a stitch that immediately laddered down many rows. "Fortunately, I had a locking stitch marker and could catch it where it was, but I was looking at a lot of picky stitch by stitch ripping back, managing two colors at once and remembering which row I was on. Even if I didn't drop other stitches along the way, the process was going to take three or four hours. I told myself *later,* shoved the whole mess in my bag, and sat there cussing myself all the way home."

Though people who don't know our craft might assume that it's only beginners or the inept who make mistakes, every one of us who regularly plies the needles knows that even the most advanced knitters mess up at least occasionally. Stitches *will* be dropped, the count *will* change by mistake as two stitches are inadvertently knit together or the plies of one are split into two; rows *will* be miscounted in patterns or cables *will* be crossed in the wrong direction; errors will disrupt lace or color patterns; decreases or increases will be forgotten.

Granted, in certain cases and with the knowledge of insider techniques, experienced knitters can avoid the tedium that is stitch-by-stitch unraveling, or "ripping out." Localized glitches in colorwork can be fixed by judicious overstitching. Dropped stitches can be caught and rewoven up the rows if the light is good and the project is simple. Even if major regression is necessary, a bold knitter with steady hands can take a deep breath and, in a context where she won't be disturbed, C-A-R-E-F-U-L-L-Y take the project off the needles, lay it on a flat surface, pull the yarn out gently row by row through where the problem occurred, then return the stitches to the needles.

In the case of more complex patterns and nastier boo boos, though, even the experts among us are doomed to the tedious process of progressive unmaking as we pass the briefly-liberated loops of each previous row backwards from one needle to the other. Ripping out is a miserable procedure—at once boring and demanding of intense attention—whose slang name, "frogging," suggests the low esteem in which it's held.

Yet this recursive tedium is such a common feature of our craft that a widely-repeated aphorism holds "Knitters are rippers." Another (as anyone who has ever belonged to a knitting group or taught or owned a shop will know) is "Knitters are people who try to talk themselves out of ripping." You can tell a lot about a knitter's personality, in fact, by the strategy her inner dialogue takes.

At one extreme is the subspecies of blithe, slapdash practitioners (full disclosure: my own native disposition tends in this direction). When we speedy ones realize that we've a mistake, we reach instinctively for denial. *This isn't all that bad,* we tell ourselves. *It won't show, and nobody will notice. Just go on knitting—don't waste time going back.*

An opposing tribe consisting of more exacting or insecure knitters becomes terminally discouraged and/or daunted at any error, even a truly small one, and leans toward what might be overdramatically called "knitting euthanasia." Deconstructing the whole piece and starting over is absolutely required, they tell themselves; the mistake can in no way be satisfactorily repaired by partial ripping or patching.

If ultimately translated into action rather than momentarily flirted with, these are both counterproductive strategies, of course. We trimmers ultimately know in our hearts that the holes or botched stitches are likely to show—and experience quickly teaches us that by some nasty cosmic law they'll almost certainly end up on the most public surface of the piece. The error may mess with fit, too, and that, along with the fact that we'll always be aware of the compromising spots even if others don't notice them, means that we'll be much less likely to wear/use the object once it's completed.

Those who incline toward knitting euthanasia court a different kind of fall. If the project has progressed very far, when completely unraveled it will constitute a dauntingly-sized ball (or for those so demoralized they don't rewind as they go, a tangled mess on the floor) that physically emblemizes wasted effort. Moreover, if the discouraged one is a true knitter she'll already have wonderful new projects lined up and waiting, virgin yarn she's yearning to pass through her fingers. The current enterprise may well be put "temporarily" aside as she turns to something new for a little break—and we all know what's likely to be its fate, stored out of sight and mind in a yarn stash, its raw materials eternally tainted with a whiff of failure.

Ripping out is thus an inevitable discipline for knitters who desire happy satisfaction in (or even completion during the current decade of) their work, an admittedly frustrating fundamental of our craft. Yet it, too, invites us along the path to spiritual growth.

Most simply and obviously, ripping out schools us in personal humility and patience—crucial life-lessons that other aspects of the craft also teach, albeit with less brutal clarity. It reminds us of the folly of imagining ourselves as perfect and self-sufficient experts; when a knitter discovers that she must go backwards, she is forced to acknowledge that she has something new to master about technique and/or about her own distractible mind. To prevent recurrences, she is invited to cultivate proactive strategies whose relevance extends far beyond knitting: swallowing her pride and consulting someone farther along the path for guidance, critically examining her own behavior to identify what led to the problem, learning from her mistakes.

A variant phrasing of the aphorism mentioned above can take us farther than mere self-correction, though, siting needlework failures in the broad context of general human nature and behavior patterns. "All good knitters are good rippers," this common alternative goes.

This difference in phrasing may seem minor, but it bears profound implications, since coupling "all" with "knitters" and "rippers" emphasizes that the chronic making of mistakes is not an individual's unique problem, the consequence of some fundamental personal inadequacy or perverse disposition. Human beings, the underlying claim of this version suggests, cannot avoid making mistakes, since human nature is innately imperfect.

That such a thing might be said about us mortals in general will certainly come as no revelation to anybody who has chosen to read a book with "spiritual" in its title. Whether human fallibility is attributed to original sin or characterized as an innate tendency to go astray or explained by the nature of reality or past-life misbehavior or past trauma in this life, it's a timeless theological/philosophical/psychoanalytical truism. It's also a paradoxically life-giving one. If we grant that everybody inevitably messes up in attempting the more general business of moving ethically, lovingly, and reverently around the world each day, it becomes absurd to hold ourselves to a standard of always-perfect behavior or to impose such a standard on others. *Of course* we should always try to live in accord with principles we understand to be holy. But cultivating a habit of self-forgiveness can help us persist after localized failures rather than lapsing into defeatism. Perfectionism, after all, as extensive clinical research has demonstrated, fosters guilt, lack of self-esteem, isolation from others, depression, and suicidal thoughts—all conditions pretty much guaranteed to sully both our souls and our conduct.

So important is forgiveness for spiritual (and psychological, and physical) health that wisdom traditions worldwide have posed it as a core tenet. The divine nature itself is widely held to be merciful and forgiving. Even the Old Testament God relents after the flood and keeps his rainbow pact never to destroy the earth again, forgiving the Israelites time after time even when any rational being (as we humans understand the term, at least) would have cut losses and moved on from the experiment in creation. "Indeed, Allah forgives all sins," the Quran reassures believers (39:53). Divine understanding of human frailty is a constantly-repeated trope in Jesus's teaching; it is also featured in Krishna's discourse in the Bhagavad-Gita.

For our part, we mortals have little alternative but to rely on this ever-flowing mercy, acknowledging our errors and performing penance for them—whether literally fabricated by our own knitting hand or introduced metaphorically in the interpersonal fabric of a knitting circle.

It's not enough, though, just to make a gesture. To achieve reconciliation with the incarnational divine, we practitioners must make a good confession, one marked by humility and active penance. The 1647 Westminster Confession, foundational in many Protestant denominations, offers a benchmark definition: the believer "grieves for and hates his or her sins" and "turns from them all unto God" (15.2).

Cultivating the practice of making "good confessions," which starts with admitting that we have made a mistake, is fundamental for any knitter who wishes to obtain God's mercy and go on with her task at hand—with yarn, children, jobs, or anything else we are trying to do well. We simply cannot hope to be truly good at *anything* unless we have learned to be good at making amends.

Questions for Reflection or Discussion

1. Name three other things you try to do perfectly in your life that you regularly have to go back and redo (e.g. raising orchids...or children). How does it feel *when* you do go back? How does it feel *after* you redo what you did? Give an example.
2. How do you react when you discover you have knitted a mistake? What other reactions might you develop when this inevitability occurs? Be specific.
3. Can ripping be as spiritual as knitting? Explore your answer.

So Many Good Ways to Knit

The Path of Sacred Individuality

Though Anna and Liz are close friends and both very skilled knitters, their philosophies and practice could hardly be more different. Anna is exacting, the sort of knitter who not only makes gauge swatches and blocks them before measuring but also considers seaming an interesting art. She loves complicated kits (among her favorite designers are Kaffe Fawcett and Alice Starmore), and she craves numerically-exact elements when she crafts her own designs, including entrelac and complex Aran cables. Anna's pieces are stunning: precisely stitched, impeccably fitting, so professional-looking they might have come from a couturier's line.

Liz, on the other hand, is a splash-and-dash knitter, a free spirit who appears constitutionally incapable of following a pattern to the letter. She designs on the fly rather than carefully charting, simply ripping out and re-knitting if she doesn't like the result until she's satisfied. Her gauge is loose and, rather than swatching over and over to get the exact number of stitches per inch noted on a pattern, Liz adjusts with expedients that make Anna shiver a little. At the moment, for example, Liz is knitting an "extra small" sweater for herself that promises to fit her substantial body just fine. And it will.

Nevertheless, both women's work draws much admiration and has won sweepstakes ribbons at the Idaho State Fair.

There are some obvious explanations for their different styles, of course. Anna is a mathematics professor and a Midwesterner of very orderly domestic habits; she possesses a brilliant logical mind ideally suited to proofs (and entrelac).

Liz, in contrast, teaches in the humanities, where the questions asked in analysis are assumed to have no singular correct answers and writing is often speculative. She grew up in the more improvisational culture of an eastern metropolis, and her housekeeping is pleasantly relaxed. Anna's a practical Taurus; Liz is a free-flowing double Gemini.

But the two of them don't care about reasons for their diversity. Absolutely comfortable with each other, they knit, talk, and visit yarn stores together, each smiling at the other's predictability, each admiring the other's style even as she happily embraces her own.

"No law can be sacred to me but that of my own nature," advised nineteenth-century American writer and Transcendentalist philosopher Ralph Waldo Emerson, voicing a sentiment obviously relevant to Anna and Liz...and to you and me.

Of Puritan stock and a clergyman's son, Emerson began his adult work in the way his family expected, becoming a minister in his twenties and assuming leadership of one of the most venerable churches in Boston in 1829. After just a few years, however, his path took a sharp turn when he broke with organized religion, convinced that *all* formal religious sects imposed improper limits on spiritual life. "The relations of the soul to the divine spirit are so pure that it is profane to seek to interpose helps," he wrote in his famous essay "Self- Reliance."

Emerson became a famous visionary and reformer, one whose ideas deeply influenced American assumptions about freedom of thought. "Trust thyself," he wrote. "Every heart vibrates to that iron string." He cautioned against blind adherence to the past's creeds and conformity to peer pressure, holding that each person's true and distinctive inner nature is a direct gift from the divine, "the essence of genius, of virtue, and of life."

To be true to your individual gifts without self-doubt or apology, Emerson insisted, is to be open to discovering and to fulfilling the purpose for which you've been created.

Christians may well hear a Biblical echo of Emerson's thought in Saint Paul's first letter to the Corinthians: "There are different kinds of spiritual gifts but the same Spirit…different workings but the same God who produces them in everyone" (I Corinthians 12: 4-7). The divine needs diverse talents, Paul suggests as he evokes the well-known metaphor of our individual gifts as parts of a body. Whether we operate like "hands," or "feet," or "eyes," or "ears," we all have our own crucially distinctive work to do and ways to do it, and we should not feel superior or inferior to the others as we knit along our individual spiritual paths.

"Who exactly am I?" can be a challenging question, one that requires many years of exploration as we grow through myriad changes. Children and adolescents often try to define themselves by simple external markers (*I always wear yellow. I'm the boy who lives for soccer.*) Young adults—and sometimes older adults who still like easy answers—adopt ready-made roles (*I'm the angst-ridden writer. I'm the self-sacrificing dad. I'm the sad-but-merry widow or divorcée.*)

Most of us, though, are engaged in a life-long quest to understand our messy, often contradictory selves. We might take personality tests, either in the context of school or a job or voluntarily, learning that we are, say, Meyers-Briggs ENTPs or Enneagram 4s. The results are said to indicate our innate strengths and weaknesses, to suggest occupations more or less congenial (e.g., introverts probably shouldn't become public relations officers) and even to provide insight into our spiritual natures, gifts, and weak points.

Any knitter with like-minded friends enjoys an additional, less category-bound source of self-knowledge thanks to the opportunity to compare her techniques and style preferences with those of others. One person in a knitting group might always seem to be working with bright, cheerful colors, whereas a second knitter's choices are habitually subdued light browns, grays, and creams. Some gravitate toward long-term projects like afghans; others prefer the stimulation of a series of quick knits.

"What an unusual cast-on that is—way over my head!" or "You're knitting that sweater side-to-side, aren't you? Wow, that's interesting!" Such apparently mundane observations can teach us a lot about our companions and about ourselves. If you're the person who always admires others' complex garments but keeps knitting simple scarves, for example, you might be risk-averse. Or perhaps you're instead manifesting realistic boundaries: your skill set isn't ready yet or your life at this point is so full of stressors that what you need from knitting right now is no-brainer relaxation. If, on the other hand, you're that person who immediately tries whatever new thing the group's most advanced practitioner is doing, you might be demonstrating a high degree of confidence and laudable curiosity—or perhaps even a little recklessness.

The key to making such comparative musings constructive tools for healthy self-knowledge (rather than petty world-of-comparison judgments) is to keep them descriptive instead of self-castigating. Sure, there are objectively better and worse ways of knitting, and sure, we should learn from each other. But if you believe Emerson and Saint Paul, it would be a mistake to try to swerve from the essence of our individual genius, virtue, and life just to knit a better sweater or—even worse—be noticed for knitting a better sweater. This would be a blow not just to our individual sense of comfortable fit in the world but also to the world itself, which needs each of our unique way of being...and knitting.

That we don't all have to be alike as knitters is a message especially important for us older knitters, who grew up before the free-for-all myriad options of knitting styles now available on Ravelry and You-Tube. In our youth knitting had decided rights and wrongs, and many of us are still apt under certain circumstances to hear the echoes of a knitting teacher's long-ago judgments: *Blue and green don't go together! That gauge doesn't match the ball-band—it's WRONG! Raglan sleeves are for sloppy people who don't really care how to knit—real knitters always set in sleeves.*

Perhaps the stubbornest and most persistent of those old shibboleths is the question of which hand holds the working yarn. Are you a "thrower" (a Continental/American-style knitter who holds working yarn in her right hand) or a "picker" (an English-style knitter who uses her left)? Both have objective advantages and disadvantages, yet pervasive folklore in the United States still considers the right-handed technique to be déclassé, a beginner's style. Those who attend national knitting conferences may still occasionally encounter old-style teachers who insist that throwers "fix" their style, claiming that anyone who knows can see the sad difference such barbarian fumbling makes in the finished fabric.

Fortunately for all of us who lurk in the throwing shadows (a majority of American knitters, a fact that may comfort you), even that picker-thrower decision is gradually losing its power to shame, as one of my friends discovered during a weekend knitting retreat run by one of the country's pre-eminent designer-teachers.

The revelation came during the very first evening's session, as students learned a fancy braided cast-on. Their instructor, famous for popularizing the Eastern European tradition to which it belonged, had taught the participants with skillful patience, but still a full hour had passed before everyone "got" the complex three rows necessary.

"Great!" The encouragement came warmly. "You're all doing so well! Now just knit plain stockinet for five rows, and then take a break."

One student couldn't help but say what everybody was thinking. "It's so nice to be able to relax a little and just knit!" she exclaimed.

Everybody looked at the student and grinned. Abruptly her smile faded as she looked down at her working hands and their gaze followed. "Oh no! Now I can't hide it," she said apologetically. "I'm a thrower. I'm so embarrassed."

"Don't worry about it!" The voice was their instructor's. "I throw a lot of the time, too."

Gasps of surprise ensued, and in response the woman told a "me-too" story. A few years earlier she'd sat waiting for a plane and knitting. "So," she recounted, "I'm really concentrating on these socks I'm designing for a yarn manufacturer—not even aware I'm throwing because I'm so wrapped up in the decisions I'm having to make. An older woman sits down next to me, and she's nice. Pretty soon, though, I see her peeking over at me, and then she starts to make little faces, and I think *Oh, oh, something's coming.*"

Finally the interloper could no longer contain herself. "Oh, that's really beautiful!" she announced to this knitting superstar. "But you're doing it wrong, dear!"

Now laughter as bright as the breaking of new light rang out in the class.

"So, what I'd tell you," the instructor continued, "is that nobody has the right to make you feel second-rate about how you knit. If there's something that works for you, use it whenever you can. That's part of who you are as an individual knitter."

She spread her hands wide, air-embracing them all. "And isn't it wonderful," she exclaimed, "that there are so many good ways to do things?"

Questions for Reflection or Discussion

1. Name some things, outside of knitting, you do differently from some or most other people (e.g., use a knife or

scissors, cook or eat a meal, raise a kid, read a book). Now think about what ways are your knitting styles, practices, and processes differ from those of some other knitters you know. Make a list of positive things you learn about yourself (and others) from watching people do things differently from you.

2. Name three things you have observed from your own experience or observing others that came about from people thinking or acting independently. Don't be afraid to use historical examples.
3. Think about a friend who differs from you in how she does something specific. Note how her distinctive approach enables her to make different choices than you might do or have done. If possible, have a conversation with her about what you like about (or have learned from) the way she does things (including knitting, if applicable).

"And the World Will Live as One"

The Path of Cross-Cultural Understanding

The woman stopped to pick us up that August afternoon in the remote North Atlantic Faroe Islands, after we'd gotten turned around on our hike and rejoined the road miles from where we'd left our rental car. In that lightly-populated land, with its mountains and fjords and vast open spaces, people look out for each other, and though she had to make a detour to take us back to town she insisted.

"What are you doing in the islands?" she asked, and we told her about the ten-day knitting workshop we were attending and the pleasure we were discovering in Faroese knitting. She nodded, smiling at our enthusiasm. Then, growing thoughtful, she volunteered, "I think I'm about the only woman here who doesn't really like to knit—though I've certainly done plenty of it."

When she was a girl growing up in the 1950s, she explained, her fisherman father had perished at sea as so many Faroese have done over the centuries, leaving her mother with seven children to support. The family possessed no savings, and so her mother, grandmother, and she (the oldest child at eleven) had gone to work "knitting for a third": that is, contracting themselves to knit for a store and receiving a third of the eventual sale price in bartered household goods. "We knit our fingers ragged. After I came home from school, I'd knit into the night by oil lamps because we didn't have electricity back then." Such craft-labor was an essential supplement to the odd jobs the family did, she told us proudly, and thanks to the knitting the children were all able to finish their schooling. Our new friend even attended college to become an accountant.

"The things we made were beautiful," she reminisced. "And everything our family ever achieved was because of knitting. But you know, since I grew up and went away to school knitting has just never been something I've been eager to do again."

In the developed western world of the twenty-first century, it's very tempting to romanticize "folk knitting," or "traditional peasant knitting." We who live in our urbanized, pre-fab, bustling postmodern era—where we have so little time to knit

compared to what we'd like—might even envy those imagined knitters of long ago and far away who created beautiful intricate designs, picturing them knitting on peaceful fireside evenings while children played and pretty little cows grazed outside on the heather.

Those of us who are comparatively rootless might also envy the cultural continuity we imagine they must have enjoyed as they learned the gorgeous colorwork on those Latvian mittens, say, from family transmission stretching back into the mists of history.

It's sweet, certainly, to imagine such an idyllic past for knitting. But that Faroese woman's real-life experience—and indeed the historically-documented experience of many traditional knitters in the past—stands in stark contrast to many of our romantic fabrications. Their reasons for knitting were often pragmatic, their lives usually hard.

Such facts might on the surface seem to open a chasm of strangeness between us knitters today and our foremothers.

Yet knowledge like this is exactly what we spiritually-minded knitters—we who aspire to the cross-cultural human understanding and harmony so necessary for human evolution—should seek. As long as we are content to make up fanciful stories about "others," after all, we have no possibility of really knowing them. Only as we open to seriously learning about them and encountering their differences will we see them in all their complexity, honoring them as the multi-faceted human beings they are and discarding the easy stereotypes. Then—and only then—will we have a chance of appreciating the wonder of how alike all we knitters really are. We are children of the same divine spirit, despite the varied circumstances of our lives.

Thus those of us who dream, in the words of John Lennon, that "someday the world will live as one," would do well to begin with a little self-education about the history of our craft.

If there's one basic fact about knitting in previous centuries and places you should know, it's this: the vast majority of our predecessors were knitting for their lives and their families' lives, just like that Faroese woman my friends and I met not too long ago. There were exceptions, of course. For example, women of leisure knit for fulfillment; young girls in comfortable households learned knitting as a womanly virtue; highly skilled craftspeople (especially the members of elite men's guilds) found prestige and wealth in the craft.

Most people in the past, however, knit because they had to. They knit utilitarian garments to keep themselves and their families warm, shaping essential hats, scarves, socks, vests, sweaters, even underwear. They knit constantly, sometimes multi-tasking. Old photographs show people knitting outdoors as they tend sheep, elderly people knitting while minding babies, girls knitting as they read schoolbooks, people knitting as they ride horses or donkeys or walk from one place to another.

By the 1600s, hand-knitting had become a cottage industry, with 200,000 people knitting socks commercially in England. Danes, Eastern Europeans, and Spaniards knit for export; Icelandic, Shetland, and Faroese knitters sold garments to the whalers and traders who visited their islands. On a more local scale, servants knit both practical garments and fancywork for grand households and courts across Europe and black enslaved people knit for their plantation owners in the American South.

Knitting soon became established as a way for those with few opportunities to make a modest living. Girls in British Victorian poorhouses and penitentiaries were taught to knit; after the potato famine, the Irish poor were instructed by a government agency in knitting Aran sweaters for sale in the United

States. Catholic nuns taught First-Nations peoples in the Pacific Northwest to knit in the late nineteenth century, accurately anticipating that bourgeoning white settlement would erode traditional ways of life.

In Sweden, halfway across the world and half a century later, Emma Jacobsson, a governor's wife, established a cooperative cottage industry that became world-famous for its distinctive designs called *Bohus Stickning* that provided income for unemployed stonecutters and their families in the remote province of Bohuslän.

Knitting for commercial markets was and remains demanding. "Speed was an issue," writes knitting historian Lela Nargi. Those who produced the most products in the least amount of time made the most money and were the most respected (an echo of this sentiment is retained in the friendly competitions Shetlanders undertake to see who is "the world's fastest knitter"). Fingers blistered; eyesight dimmed; hand, arm, and shoulder muscles cramped with all that repetitive motion, and back/hip muscles tightened and spasmed with all that sitting. To make a mistake and rip wasn't just an annoyance but a potential economic disaster. To produce something of inferior quality and have it rejected might mean your family going hungry.

Even delivering the finished products to market could be taxing. Knitters in the Cornwall village of Looe, for example, carried 8-10 heavy fisherman's sweaters each on their backs twenty miles over the hills to Plymouth. And the compensation for everyone—as is so typical in the case of cottage-industry pieceworkers—represented only a fraction of the labor's worth.

So, yes, those old-time knitters were actually very different than us, and hardly the stuff of sentimental dioramas.

Nevertheless, knitting is knitting, and so it's possible through the happy medium of our shared craft to imagine some common elements of our foremothers' experience. Like us, they may have thought about their loved ones in the quiet that knitting brings, mused about the future and reflected on the past, just as we do today. Those long-ago and far-away knitters would also have enjoyed the anticipatory sense of beginning that casting on brings, the satisfied completion of casting off, and the deep pleasure in a piece that turned out well. Interacting with neighbors in a cooperative (or with brokers or storekeepers while delivering their work) might have relieved rural loneliness, just as modern knitting groups draw us from our computers into human fellowship.

Like us, those piecework knitters would have been invited (or required) to develop new or better skills, struggling with self-doubt and temporary frustrations as they labored to get a new technique right, to comprehend unfamiliar principles of design and sizing and finishing. When they mastered something, they must have felt a happy burst of self-satisfaction similar to what we feel today, and the successful among them would have stood a little taller thanks to the respect of their peers, just as we stand tall when people admire our work.

Like us, too, knitters then were invited to explore the depths of their own creativity. That might sound like romantic speculation, given the pressures they faced, but it's not. Knitting historians have documented interesting, even radical evolution in local market-knitting traditions over time, apparently driven by grassroots practitioners as somebody got a good idea and others copied her and then experimented with their own riffs.

Knitters have always been borrowers, it appears, and just because you're knitting fast and commercially doesn't mean you abandon your imagination. Those Cowichan Indian women in the Pacific Northwest transformed the Fair Isle yokes they learned from white knitters into their signature regional style, swapping out geometric grids for images of moose, eagles, and bears. Scandinavian, Icelandic, Faroese, and Shetland knitters stole colorways and pattern elements from one another and from the Balkan styles worn by visiting traders. Ingenious Russian knitters devised a pretty variation in their lace "wedding-ring" Orenburg shawls that paid a literal dividend, adding *nupps* (bobbles) which boosted the shawl's weight (an historical criterion for pricing).

Thus knitting, while an arduous way to make a living, helped women over history survive but also discover who they were, just as it does today.

Anyone concerned with social justice—that is to say, anyone on a spiritual path—needs to be aware that "others" who are knitting for a living still exist around the world today. South American women are hand-knitting in hopes of alleviating crushing poverty, tweaking traditions in color and pattern to satisfy modern tastes and their own creative instincts. Women are even now piecework-knitting for the tourist trade in Scotland, Ireland, Wales, Iceland, and the islands off Britain and Scandinavia—often still selling their beautiful handiwork to stores or brokers for a pittance of what it's worth. People in many countries are designing patterns, doing basic or art knitting, spinning and dyeing yarn, and raising fiber animals as their primary means of support rather than as an indulgent hobby, and many of them work on very tight margins. So, if you're a person committed to supporting the sisterhood of knitters, you should consider buying their wares as directly from them as humanly and humanely possible.

It's true that seeking out artisan-knit items can be more time-consuming than buying from a third-party broker, and handmade and individually designed pieces are often now more expensive than factory-produced imitations. Yet, in my opinion, supporting grassroots knitters is the right thing to do, for it affirms not just the craft we share but our common spirit as well.

Even while acknowledging our differences, we can admire the skill, wonder at the persistence, pity the sorrow, and smile to imagine the triumphs of those who knit for a living. We can hold them in our hearts, as if they were our sisters.

Questions for Reflection or Discussion

1. Have you ever met a knitter from another culture, including someone of a different social class, ethnicity, or race? Tell that story. What did you find you had in common, and what differences?
2. Name a folk-knitting tradition you are interested in or have heard about. Take the time to look up more information about its history and practice, and then share it with others with whom you knit.

3. Do you agree that romanticizing (or assuming things) about the life experience of people who knit or produce fiber/yarn for a living can interfere with fruitful, respectful connection with them? If so, what are you going to do about it?

Knitting and Nature

The Path of Awareness and Celebration

If knitting could be said to have shrines, the building where Jamieson's of Shetland yarn is manufactured would surely be among them. Getting there arguably counts as a pilgrimage, anyway; you fly an hour north from Edinburgh to the Shetland archipelago, then drive west-northwest for longer than that on winding two-track (sometimes one-track) roads to the remote community of Sandness on the far west coast of the main island.

But what a sight greets you in the shop! An entire long wall of cubbies displays every single color—more than 220 shades—of the world-famous yarn made at this mothership and celebrated by those who love traditional fiber and color-work. Forget about "blue" and "brown," "red" and even "white." Each cubby holds a subtle grouping: more greenish vs more bluish teals, whites with grey tones vs whites with ecru ones, reds that shade from hinting at purple to almost purple. It's as if those paint chip cards in hardware stores transformed themselves into yarn.

The sight is glorious...and overwhelming. Knitters lucky enough to visit (as part of a group or by arrangement only) tend to linger for a very long time, rethinking what they really want, after all, in the face of so many possibilities. I'm embarrassed to admit my friend Sarah and I spent more than two hours deciding what to buy the day we visited Jamieson's, eventually leaving that fiber-arts Lourdes with multiple comically-stuffed shopping bags apiece.

We hadn't planned to spend so much of our precious day shopping—we're not "that kind of people." In the end, though, we gained happy food for thought about how yarn-people think, as well as some good swag. As the numbers of skeins we examined and exclaimed over multiplied, the essential depth of connection between this particular spot on Earth and these yarn makers came home to us. Every one of those colors is named for a feature of the landscape. "Bramble," one skein band read; "wren," another; "highland mist" a third. "Sunrise" was different than "sunset;" local dialect names for subtly-gradated sheep colors distinguished "eesit" from "mooskit;" hundreds of names of the material spoke of observation so close and loving it bordered on reverence.

It seems obvious to proclaim that, in a very fundamental sense, knitters are practicing a *natural* craft. Unless you knit

with acrylic 100% of the time, in which case...well, let's not go there...the yarns you use come from animals and plants, no matter what their colors or texture are called.

If you're a true knitting enthusiast, you're likely to have traveled at some point or other to meet some of those animals in person at a farm or fiber fair: adorable (though feisty) alpacas, sweetly bleating cashmere goats, fluffy angora rabbits, sheep in myriad colors being herded in a field by a professional dog with eyes so focused the gaze seems a little crazy. You might know the difference between the more obvious breeds of those sheep: sturdy Rambouillets; Lincolns with their long, almost-corded fleece; Icelandic sheep looking like enormous dandelions on the hillsides; tiny, sturdy true Shetland sheep; Navajo Churros with their distinctive curling horns—and you may have even sought out breed-specific wool.

You'll likewise get a little picky about the sourcing of your cotton. If you see a blue flax plant growing in your yard, you can catch yourself thinking, *Gee, if I had enough of that, I could make linen yarn.* You'll also consider wooden needles as art objects and perhaps develop a preference for rosewood over brazilwood (though you may find metal or composite ones easier to use), and you will delight in stitch markers with dangling gemstones (though likely you'll actually use utilitarian ones with nothing to get tangled).

Beyond materials, the objects we make sometimes feature literal pictures of natural objects. Sheep (how meta is that?), rabbits, goats, even musk-oxen show up on the yokes of sweaters or the backs of mittens. Kids' garments reflect the recipient's preference for doggies, kitties, or whales. Flowers, too, make their appearance both in abstracted geometrical patterns and in entrelac pictures of, say, a giant calla lily. Lace shawls depict trees whose size shrinks or grows in repeated bands as the garment's dimensions change.

Some natural motifs are specifically associated with local environments, like Cowichan bears and Norwegian representations of reindeer and bright northern stars. What memorable local references have you put into or seen in a finished piece?

The dyes that historically made color-knitting possible came from natural, though not always romantic, sources (one common bright red, cochineal, originates from crushed-up bugs). Even today individual enthusiasts and small yarn producers take pride in natural dyeing. For example, the folks at Tierra Wools in New Mexico, whose yarn is spun from local Churros, color their fiber with shades derived from black walnut, madder, juniper, mistletoe, and acorns, among other things.

It can't be an accident, either, that so many yarn producers and shops are located in scenic places. True, you need to be in the country to have sheep, but not necessarily in *inspirationally-beautiful* country. Tierra Wools' setting on the Brazos in the northern New Mexico mountains exemplifies this, as does Churchmouse Yarn's on Washington State's Bainbridge Island, as does the wind-swept setting of Jamieson's of Shetlands' spinnery in Sandness, etc. Shops in more pedestrian urban settings often do their best at providing an inspirationally-beautiful environment with plants and big windows whose natural light makes the colors of the yarn inside glow.

Naturally beautiful, too, are the settings for so many of our knitting classes and retreats. Businesspeople might be content to do in-service training in nondescript hotel conference rooms (or worse, via Zoom), but aside from mega-conventions we knitters definitely prefer to meet up in landscapes that make our souls soar. If you're a knitter with means, you can hone your craft in the red rock country of Arizona, on the Maine coast, or in the Colorado mountains. If staying closer to home or budget is your style, you can join knitting friends in the community green spaces or state parks that can be found virtually everywhere.

If you're a knitter who's all-in with the premise of this book, you can even attend a knitting retreat at a monastery or abbey. In such instances—at Waltham Abbey in Essex, England, say, or at the Benedictine Monastery of St. Gertrude in Cottonwood, Idaho—attendees are invited to talk about the connections between knitting and spiritual life and to sample the observances and reverent focus of their hosts. Such retreats typically afford abundant opportunities for refreshing the soul in nature, too, via taking breaks to stroll peaceful grounds or participate in contemplative knitting sessions that invite you to watch passing clouds and listen to singing birds as you work by a window or on a garden bench.

Monastery grounds, in fact, offer an especially accessible example of what Celtic spirituality called "thin places". These are locations where the boundaries between Heaven and Earth are particularly permeable and a person can more easily sense the divine presence in our world.

You don't need to go to such a formal sacred place, though, to feel a spontaneous up-welling of reverence for and identity with nature. As knitters of a spiritually reflective disposition are probably already aware, such joyful, awe-inducing flashes of insight can happen just about anywhere, especially when you find yourself outside and alone. Ancient and medieval people—including those Celts—knew that too; they took it for granted that the entire natural world crackled with *animation* (in the strict sense, "containing a spirit or life-force").

Though Christianity was notorious for attempting to quash such "pagan" sensibilities, animistic reverence for nature never went away. In the seventeenth century, it resurfaced in the work of philosophers, including Spinoza and Rousseau, who proclaimed the immanence of the divine force in creation and the natural world's power to help us connect with our own transcendent nature.

Generations of writers and artists embraced this theme, among them English poet William Wordsworth, who chronicled spiritual epiphanies in the mountains; and American naturalist/conservationist John Muir, who asserted that trees' "songs never cease." Twenty-first-century "green" spiritualities affirm such animism, considering the Earth to be a living being and insisting (as Native American spirituality has always done) that humans are not dualistically separated from nature but part of an integral whole. As the effects of global warming have become more obvious, Christianity too has leaned toward eco-spirituality, for example with Pope Francis' encyclical *Laudato Si*'s vision of "integral ecology."

If you believe that mystery is immanent in the natural world, as the eco-spirituality that informs all of these voices holds, then noticing and appreciating the details of that sphere can become *worship*, "a primary practice of spiritual life," as one contemporary commentator puts it.

And that insight has especially happy implications for us knitters who seek the path of spiritual enlightenment, for our craft necessarily makes us into world-class noticers of the natural world. By implication, every morning as we linger knitting in the back yard with coffee and take the time to notice a hummingbird darting to feed in the lilacs, or when we see a sheep grazing by the road and think, "Wow, she has Merinos," or even as we remember wrens we've seen as we pick up that wren-colored yarn—we're engaging in a spiritual act. We're becoming people primed with open eyes, you might say, to celebrate the world's beauty and diversity, knitters inclined through the work of our hands to gratitude and joyful celebration of the incredible abundance that surrounds us.

"Ever since I went to Jamieson's and started knitting with that yarn," Sarah says, "I've seen color differently. There aren't any generic trees for me anymore; I'm constantly noticing the variations—Ponderosa Pines versus Spruce versus Junipers. I've always loved nature, but I actually think I'm better at appreciating it now. And it's sure easier for me now to identify plants, crops, and wildflowers."

"I know just what you mean," Anna replies. She gestures to the mountain ridge where the three of us sit taking a break on this early-summer hike, at the blue-purple Lupines, red Indian Paintbrush, and yellowish-white flowers of Rabbitbrush blooming together on the sweeping open slope we're about to ascend. "This is sort of like hiking through an Alice Starmore sweater."

She sips her water and considers. "But not quite. If I were going to design an Eastern Idaho sweater, there'd have to be more pale sage in it, a little of that Slate Mountain slate. No ocean blue, but *this* sky and *those* clouds."

Sarah and I smile, guessing what's coming next.

"Maybe I'll fool around with that tomorrow," Anna muses. "Why should Scotland have all the glory? A lot of people think Idaho isn't as pretty as where they live—well, it's about time they woke up!"

Abruptly her expression takes on a little mischief. "Can I borrow some of your pale sage yarn?" she asks us. "I'm pretty sure you both still have some left to share."

Questions for Reflection or Discussion

1. Describe a spiritual experience you have had in the natural world. Where were you, and what happened? Be specific, using concrete nouns and precise adjectives and adverbs.
2. List three ways knitting has helped you to be more aware of the world around you. (If you have never had this experience, start paying attention!) What features of nature are you more likely to notice and celebrate because of your knitting?
3. Name the most beautiful places you know well. How have you or might you incorporate them into your knitting?

“All Great Works of Art Are Annunciations”

The Path of Joyful Co-Creation

About five centuries after the image of a knitting Madonna described in this book’s introduction was painted, the British artist-engraver William Hamilton contributed his own take on the same theme to publisher Thomas Macklin’s famous *1800 Bible*.

One among seventy illustrations in this physically-enormous work, Hamilton’s image might be more accurately described as "a Madonna who knits," since its subject is much too preoccupied at the moment depicted with what is being announced to take up the needles and yarn shown in a foreground basket. Mary is caught in the midst of one of the most wonderous, ineffable events in Christian lore: the Annunciation, when the Angel Gabriel delivers the news that, although a virgin, the young girl will bear God's son incarnate.

In recent years, the term "makers" has been employed widely in popular culture to signify and elevate those who might once have been called "crafters" or "artisans"—people who sew, knit, color fabric, design household and leisure goods, create food products and recipes, and so forth. There are now multiple contests for entrepreneurial "makers," run by everybody from Martha Stewart to Title Nine, the women's athletic wear company, that offer their winners a hand-up in transition from

"hobbyist-blogger-occasional-craft-fair-seller" to full-fledged "businessperson."

Intended to flatter craftspeople and enhance their marketing, this word "maker" also (perhaps unintentionally) carries a connotation that elevates their status in a spiritual way, one that might give a strict fundamentalist pause. In the great majority of faith traditions, as you'll know, the ultimate "Maker" is the divine, as in "it is (insert your word for the Mystery) that has made us and not we ourselves." Most creeds hold that this Uber-lifeforce isn't done making, either, continually overseeing this created world, reaching in, hearing prayers, responding to creatures, forming things. To be a human "maker" in this context, is to shine with divine creative light.

Hamilton's engraving *The Annunciation* represents a central moment for Christians of active divine intervention in the physical world. If you're familiar with the biblical narrative, you'll understand that there's a lot of "making" going on in the picture: the Divine Spirit itself has implanted seed in Mary's womb; Mary is already gestating; the Angel Gabriel is "making" the news known in his proclamation.

What's most significant for me, though, is that Mary, by the implication of those knitting needles and yarn, has even before this moment been a "maker-of-things" herself, warming up in a minor key, you might say, by turning the potential of fiber into knitted objects.

This metaphor isn't original with Hamilton; at least a dozen other artists' renderings of the Annunciation include objects related to needlework in Mary's immediate environment. Alessandro Allori, for example, shows a discarded bobbin-lace-loom on a stool; Peter Paul Rubens pictures an overflowing work basket (complete with dozing attendant cat) by the chair from which Mary's just sprung up at the angel's approach.

The framing of Mary as an active knitter in these images carries not just decorative charm but also theological implications, alerting the Christian viewer that the young Jewish girl was not a passive participant in the incarnation. Christian doctrine holds that it's crucial to understand that Mary said "Yes!" of her own free will by proclaiming, "Let it be done to me." Mary—whose inborn, ongoing capacity to create is suggested by the knitting—thus stands in Christian iconography as an exemplar who brings her own God-given creative capacity to the service of divine creativity. Such images invite believers to understand that they, too—if they can learn to hear and obey the way she does—also bear within themselves the capacity to become agents of the divine will in this world.

Leaving aside the specifically Christian theological elements, an idea very much like this animates the spiritual concept of *co-creation* so widely popular today. In a non-denominational, even non-theistic way, co-creation holds that the

Mystery of Life has formed humans with capacities that will help advance the progress of the cosmos—capacities which will allow us to be, as it were, God's working hands.

Those of us who dedicate ourselves to realizing such potential (both "realizing" as sensing/acknowledging, and "realizing" as acting in accordance with the gifts), become partners in changing the world for good, in co-creating it anew. That might mean helping others and the biosphere, or offering ideas that advance human consciousness, or drawing others into deeper knowledge of the lifeforce itself. Whatever the particular paths to which our gifts have called us, co-creative people know the joy of sacred self-actualization. We feel the fulfillment that comes with honoring our soul-purpose as we participate in the "strange partnership between a human being's labor and the mystery of inspiration," to borrow Elizabeth Gilbert's phrase.

If you're a knitter (or a painter, or a writer, or someone who likes to make up recipes or arrange flowers) someone has probably said to you, "I wish I could do something like that." Apologies inevitably follow—"But I'm just not the creative type." On occasion, these demurrers bear a whiff of self-righteous defensiveness: that crafty stuff might be all well and good for you, but I prefer to spend my time on more practical things.

But in fact such dichotomies between useful work and frivolous creation are long outdated. We've understood for decades that the ability to make non-logical intuitive leaps and see things in new ways—a standard definition of creativity—manifests itself in all realms of human activity. Books on business management, for cryin' out loud, advise executives on exploiting their own and their employees' creativity, as do books about medicine, technology, teaching, cooking, community organizing, politics...and almost every other human endeavor. On the personal front, it's become common to hear advice about "being creative" in the effort to heal a troubled relationship or improve one's childrearing skills.

A considerable body of research has confirmed that we human beings are hardwired to make innovative connections. "It's our brains doing what they do," University of Washington neuroscientist and engineer Michael Grybko affirms. According to a 2016 study conducted at the University of New South Wales, not only are intuitive leaps common but they can also lead to better insights than those offered by rational analysis. Such widespread findings only confirm what the wise ones among us have long known. We need to listen to our sudden rushes of inspiration.

"The intuitive mind is a sacred gift," Albert Einstein said, encapsulating his understanding of the wellspring of creativity. So widespread and universally-acknowledged today is the understanding that we bear mysterious ways of knowing and creating within us that, in fact, just about anybody would be hard-pressed to disagree (no matter what they believe or don't believe about religion or spirituality) with the ancient Psalmist's contention that we have all been "fearfully and wonderfully made" (139:14).

We're all "creative types." The issue comes in learning to say Mary's "Yes" to our potential without fear or embarrassment.

"All great works of art are Annunciations," the children's author Madeleine L'Engle has written in her book about human creativity. If you're a modest knitter, you may assume that this sentiment, beautiful as it is, doesn't apply to you and your "hobby." Our craft, after all, is concerned with common objects of everyday use—maybe pretty, but Earth-oriented vs Heaven-sent and definitely not "great works of art."

And you'd be right up to a point, for many of the things we form with two sticks and a string are nothing more than useful little objects. No knitter in her right mind would insist that divine inspiration is behind every utilitarian wooly ski sock, each pot scrubber formed from left-over economical yarn.

Nevertheless, we ought to embrace the fact that in making even them we've said "Yes" in our small way, and in that acceptance of risk and possibility and inspiration we've shared a touch of something of the spirit of all those knitting Madonnas in great art.

Who are we, after all, to assume *we* know the purpose of our modest making of things, given a universe where the divine reminds us daily that "As the heavens are higher than the earth, so are my ways higher than your ways, and my thoughts than your thoughts" (Isaiah 55:8). Who are we to jump so quickly to assumptions about what will and won't contribute to the "great project of human enlightenment"? For that beautiful pale-lavender baby blanket, with its cream and pale green and pink purl stripes and its cuddly texture, might help form a calm disposition in its tiny recipient, making her feel secure enough someday to travel to Mars. By some intuitive process it might sow a seed of appreciation for beauty and color that enriches all the decades of her life and all the people she nurtures or mentors. That quick worsted hat you knit for the homeless shelter might become a sign to a homeless man that the universe still cares, that love still exists, that he needs to go on living.

And remember that worldly objects aren't the only things we're knitting. As this book has suggested, we're each also knitting ourselves into the person we're meant to become. Knitting fills our heart with compassion, our life with a sense of meaning, and our soul with intimations of wonder, gratitude, and holy joy. Knitting can move us, in ways that might seem very mysterious indeed, to help make this tired old world new again.

"Prosper the work of our hands, O Lord," says the Psalmist. "Prosper the work of our hands."

Questions for Reflection or Discussion

1. Consider one experience you have had with non-rational inspiration, either as a knitter or beyond the context of knitting. How did you feel? Did you sense at any level that you were being used as "divine's hands"? Describe that feeling.
2. Has something you or a friend has knitted ever influenced someone else's life in a way more profound than was intended? Tell that story in all its glorious detail.
3. What have been some lower-case "annunciation" events or aspects of your own life that called you to listen more attentively to your potential for creativity? Describe the feeling you have when you experience or witness unexpected creativity.

Afterword

One Stitch at a Time

One of my best friends is also a dedicated knitter, and during the course of our regular long hikes one of us eventually asks the other, "What are you knitting now?" Far from being a trivial question, this topic inevitably reveals infinitely more about the other's state of mind than any previous topic of conversation—more about her current equanimity or stress, connection to others, ease in her own skin, and view of the universe.

Asking myself "what am I knitting right now" as I finish this book, I'm compelled to admit that despite localized irritations or the occasional night awake with existential angst or widow's loneliness, the primary theme of my life (and therefore my knitting) ought properly to be gratitude. During the summer just past, I've had time to design a soft cape of dusty pink, rich greens, creams that will warm and brighten the winter ahead—a project that has me counting the blessings of good teachers and of a trip to a distant country where that gorgeous yarn originated.

I've just completed a fancy scarf for an editor who's guided me through three books I wasn't sure I could write. I'm nearly finished with a lace-yoke custom baby dress donated as a promise to a breast-cancer benefit auction last June. Christmas knitting begins this weekend as I travel with the former graduate student who's become my "daughter" for a cabin get-away in the eastern Montana mountains. She'll see me starting a gift-to-be honeycomb cowl made with jewel-colored, hand-painted silk-merino sock yarn from a small woman-owned business I've admired for forty years, located just a few valleys away from where that cabin sits. What she won't see is my silent cogitation of an original colorway of blues, greens, browns for a much more elaborate Christmas Fair Isle cowl for her, to be begun after we return home from our trip.

How could I ever feel lonely, really, when such a litany of knitting projects demonstrates how deeply woven-in I am to this web of friends, to the glorious Intermountain-West landscape I'm blessed to inhabit? How could I ever doubt that some Mystery loves me when it's led me to this beloved, ever-developing, and infinitely interesting craft that so richly feeds my longing for beauty, for growth? This *sacred* craft, I might even insist, as conjured by the knitting Madonnas referenced earlier in this book.

Such happy gratitude does not mean, of course, that I don't and won't in future discover that I've dropped plenty of stitches—both literally and figuratively. It doesn't promise that I'll never again face the discouragement (ditto) of having to rip out and begin again. But armed with my ample craft-based practice in starting over and designing on the fly, I now find it much easier to trust in the righteousness of eventual outcomes.

What's on your needles right now? What does it say about where you are in your life's journey? How might it inspire you, as a creator yourself, to celebrate the goodness of this created world?

About the Author and the Images

Susan H. Swetnam is a lifelong knitter, knitting teacher, and pattern-tweaking designer. While her current passion is stranded colorwork, she's also a particular fan of Aran and lace knitting. A retired academic, Susan is the author of more than a dozen books, including the National Catholic Book Award-winning *In the Mystery's Shadow: Reflections on Caring for the Elderly and Dying* (2019). Her essays and articles have appeared in national magazines (*Gourmet, Mademoiselle, St. Anthony Messenger*), academic journals, and literary magazines. Now involved in a second-act career as a hospice massage therapist, Susan lives, knits, and writes in the mountains south of Pocatello, Idaho. She can be reached by email at swetsusa@isu.edu.

The Images:

- "Elder Hands Knitting," cover, used with permission under license from iStock.com by Getty Images (photo ID:865586618). All rights reserved.
- "Knitting Madonna" (also known as "The Buxtehude Altar, Right Wing" and "Visit of the Angel"), page 3, painting by Master Bertram of Minden, Germany, (ca. 1400-1410 C.E.), public domain.
- "Experiments in Fair Isle Hat Design, Autumn 2019," page 15, photo by author.
- "Orenburg Lace Shawl with Grandmother's Chair," page 29, photo by author.

- “Mother Shelley and Daughter Emma Catch Up Over Knitting,” page 43, photo by author.
- “Women Knitting in Skills Development Workshop,” page 58, used with permission under license from iStock.com by Getty Images (photo ID:93472561).
- “Keeping Lara and Peter Warm in Montana,” page 71, photo by author.
- “Flora the Kitten Discovers Yarn,” page 84, photo by author.
- “Beautiful Nora, Already Stylin’ at Age Three,” page 98, photo by author.
- “Historic Croft House, Shetland Islands,” page 112, photo by author.
- “Garden Palette,” page 128, photo by author.

- "A Madonna Who Knits (The Annunciation)," engraving by British artist William Hamilton for Thomas Macklin's *Macklin Bible*, (1800 C.E.), page 141, public domain.
- "Descending Toward the Bird Cliffs, Noss Island National Nature Reserve, Shetland," opening page and page 154, photo by author.

Gift Books in This Series

The Art of Pausing
An A-Z Guide to Letting Go
An Empty Space in Your Heart
Engaging the Gifts of Growing Older
How to Avoid Burnout
Inspired Caregiving
Knitting as a Spiritual Path
Leaps of Faith
Literary Portals to Prayer
Near Occasions of Hope
The Soul of Teaching
Where God Is at Home

Advance Praise for *Knitting as a Spiritual Path*

Knitters who pursue their craft with intention and love often feel a connection to others—around the world and throughout time. These thought-provoking essays and enquiries add valuable depth to this experience of physical, psychological, and spiritual connection.

Janine Bajus, author of *The Joy of Color: Fair Isle Knitting Your Way*

Weaving words into passages as deftly as an accomplished knitter weaves her yarn, Susan Swetnam gathers threads from the world's great contemplative traditions to fashion a spiritual guidebook for knitters. *Knitting as a Spiritual Path* is a work of art and, as Swetnam quotes the children's author Madeleine L'Engle, "works of art are Annunciations." Susan Swetnam is a faithful guide to follow into a deeper exploration of this ancient art.

Michael David Sowder, author of
The Empty Boat and *Whitman's Ecstatic Union*

You don't have to be a knitter to benefit from the insights and spiritual takeaways in Susan Swetnam's engaging gift book. If the pandemic years have taught us anything, it is the importance of patience, perseverance, and taking time for the things that bring true joy to our lives—spiritual practices knitters have long known. Give it to those who are avid knitters; but give it also to yourself. Keep it by your bedside, as I intend to do, even though I have never knitted a stich!

Judith Valente, author of *The Art of Pausing* and *How to Be*